EVERYDAY FASHIONS OF THE FIFTIES

AS PICTURED IN SEARS CATALOGS

Edited and with an Introduction by
JOANNE OLIAN
Curator Emeritus, Costume Collection
Museum of the City of New York

DOVER PUBLICATIONS, INC.
Mineola, New York

Bibliographical Note

This Dover edition, first published in 2002, is a new selection of patterns from
the following Sears, Roebuck and Co. catalogs: *Spring and Summer 1950; Spring
and Summer 1951; Fall and Winter 1951; Spring and Summer 1952; Spring and
Summer 1954; Fall and Winter 1955; Fall and Winter 1957; Sears Summer Sale,
1957; Fall and Winter 1957; Fall and Winter 1958; Fall and Winter 1959.*

The catalog images within this book are reprinted by arrangement with Sears,
Roebuck & Co. and are protected under copyright. No duplication is permitted.

Library of Congress Cataloging-in-Publication Data

Everyday fashions of the fifties as pictured in Sears catalogs / edited and with an
introduction by Joanne Olian.
    p. cm.
   ISBN 0-486-42219-4 (pbk.)
    1. Costume—United States —History—20th century. 2. Fashion—United
States—History—20th century. 3. Sears, Roebuck and Company—Catalogs.
4. Nineteen fifties. I. Olian, Joanne.

GT615 .E895 2002
391'.0973'0904—dc21

                                 2002073788

Manufactured in the United States of America
Dover Publications, Inc., 31 East 2nd Street, Mineola, N.Y. 11501

INTRODUCTION

Show me the dress of a country and I can tell you its history—Anatole France

To leaf through the pages of a 1950s Sears catalog is to be transported into a Norman Rockwell vision of middle-class America with "clean-cut" young men, "ladylike" women, and "girl next door" teens. College students stroll through ivy-covered halls in blazers and Bermudas, well-girdled wives of aspiring executives dress up in hats, gloves, and high-heeled pumps, while their hatted husbands dash off to offices in suits and ties. On summer evenings they gather around the backyard barbecue, wives in capri pants, the kids in peasant blouses or Roy Rogers jeans and Davy Crockett coonskin caps. Even grandma, alias Gracious Lady, is there, growing old ever more gracefully (in dresses up to size 52) with each succeeding Sears decade. Nor are the customers who crave high fashion and find it in the catalog at a price far below that of Fifth Avenue or Paris forgotten. In short, if future historians were to reconstruct history from the pages of Sears, what they would doubtless arrive at would be nothing short of the American Dream.

Even Soviet premier Nikita Khrushchev was deeply impressed with how well dressed Americans were. When he met with Nelson Rockefeller in 1959 he was astonished that "the biggest capitalist in the world" was dressed just like everybody else. As Claudia Kidwell pointed out, "The other side of the coin was that everybody else was dressed like Rockefeller." This equality of dress is the fundamental characteristic of American clothing. In the fifties, two elements conspired to achieve its success. First, increasing prosperity propelled unprecedented numbers of Americans into the middle class, and second, manufacturing know-how and technology enabled mass-produced garments, made of newly developed easy-care synthetic fabrics, to be sold at affordable prices. Sears, with the foresight to capitalize on the demographics and the power to command the manufacturing resources was, by mid-century, the nation's largest retailer of general merchandise (selling not only apparel for the entire family but providing it with its furnishings, appliances, and sporting and entertainment paraphernalia), whose annual sales would ultimately equal one percent of the gross national product.

The number of families moving up to the middle class was increasing by over a million every year, according to *Fortune*, whose editors projected that by 1959 half the families in America would have moved up to this category. For many of them, veterans of World War II, the American Dream meant a secure job with a large corporation, marriage and a family, and a brand-new house in the suburbs, often financed by a low-rate GI mortgage. In the fifties, 13,000,000 new houses were built, many of them on the assembly line system devel-

oped by William J. Levitt, who housed 82,000 people in 17,000 single-family Cape Cod style homes in the first Levittown alone. A New York Times ad proclaimed, "All yours for $58. You're a lucky fellow, Mr. Veteran. Uncle Sam and the world's largest builder have made it possible for you to live in a charming house in a delightful community without having to pay for them with your eye teeth. . ."

This new suburban lifestyle required a new kind of wardrobe, and Sears was equal to the challenge. Along with frilly aprons they sold capri pants, sweaters, storm coats, and jeans. Men were able to buy suburban coats, sport shirts, corduroy slacks, and stylish sweaters.

Everyday dress for each sex was very different; women stayed home in what were essentially single-sex communities during the day, while their husbands, generally the sole breadwinners in the family, donned suits, ties, and the inevitable hat, for the commute to the city.

Daytime garb for the housewife, unless she was dressing for a luncheon or taking in a matinee in town, consisted of a sweater (often of washable Orlon) and skirt or pants or the ubiquitous shirtwaist dress, worn with a short "topper" or a car coat when carpooling behind the wheel of the family car. She sipped her morning coffee with neighbors in a nylon "duster," one step above a short bathrobe. Sears' fashion consultant, Mary Lewis, advised *Women's Wear Daily* that a housewife and a career girl wear very different kinds of clothes. Suburbanites "live in pants . . . when they do put on a dress it has to be very dressy . . . so reserve promotion of the oversimplified styles for city and career girls."

Evening wear presented a sharp contrast to the demure "happy housewife" image. One writer remembers, "In the daytime we wore tight, revealing sweaters, but they were topped by mincing little Peter Pan collars and perky scarves that seemed to say, 'Who, me? Why, I'm just a little girl!' At night our shoulders were naked, our breasts half-bare, the lower half of our bodies hidden in layers of tulle." If day clothes can be thought of as Doris Day or Debbie Reynolds, the intent of after-five clothes was to transform the wearer into a femme fatale along the lines of Ava Gardner, Rita Hayworth, or Dorian Leigh, the sophisticated, alluring, raven-haired model in Revlon's "Fire and Ice" ads. Fabrics were typically brocades, tulles, or velvets, and, depending on the formality of the occasion, a dress would be long or short, sleeved or strapless. There were cocktail dresses that were slightly décolleté and worn with hats and gloves, theater suits, long and short strapless evening gowns, and ball gowns. Gloves, stiletto heels, and pointed, strapless bras or waist-cinching Merry Widows were de rigeuer with such finery.

Appropriateness was the byword. In an era when wives were considered barometers indicative of their husband's ability to succeed in a corporate world, volumes were written on the subject of suitable dress and behavior for the helpmeet. Such disparate authorities as William H. Whyte, whose cogent study coined the phrase, "The Organization Man," and Anne Fogarty, the designer responsible for the doll-waisted, full-skirted, petticoated young look of the fifties, a lighthearted, Americanized version of Dior's New Look, offered sartorial advice. In a lengthy *Fortune* article based on a study of the wife's role in the social and caste system of the modern corporation, Whyte admonished: "Be attractive. There is a strong correlation between executive success and the wife's appearance." In her 1959 book, *Wife Dressing*, Mrs. Fogarty, a Coty Award winner, claimed to be first and foremost, a wife, advocating "ultrafeminine fashion." Not only did this please a husband, "it also helped his career, since in the new corporate environment a wife's appearance was an issue, especially when 'promotions to high-echelon jobs are in the offing.'" She disdained blue jeans and recommended wearing a girdle with everything. Mattel's Barbie doll, introduced in 1959, was the Fogarty look incarnate.

Togetherness, a word coined by *McCall's* magazine, defined the attitude toward family in the fifties. In the years after World War II, Americans were marrying in record numbers, and at a much younger age. By 1959, 47 percent of all brides were under nineteen and two out of three women who started college dropped out before graduation—usually to wed. They rushed to newly created suburbs to buy homes and fill them with laborsaving appliances, freezers stocked with frozen food, television sets, and most important, kids! In America, the birth rate had risen so high that by 1957 the average family consisted of 3.2 children, and it was estimated that a baby was born every seven seconds. Two doctors were household words: Dr. Seuss, author of "*The Cat in the Hat*, the children's classic that revolutionized reading," and Dr. Spock, the ultimate authority on the American family, whose *Baby and Child Care* was the mothers' gospel of the 1950s, second in sales only to the Bible. He advocated the child-centered home with an aura of warmth and security, which could be created only by stay-at-home mothers. This philosophy was emphasized by wholesome family TV shows like *Ozzie and Harriet* and *Father Knows Best*, fashioned by scriptwriters into paradigms of the ideal family and watched faithfully in the two out of three homes which boasted at least one television set.

Not surprisingly, in the early fifties issues of Sears, baby and children's clothing takes pride of place in the front pages of the catalog. Girls wore sister dresses, boys and girls wore jeans, often with Roy Rogers' imprimatur, and felt circle skirts with poodles, later to become a cliché for nostalgic fifties parties garb, were ubiquitous. Subteen, preteen, and teen categories occupied steadily increasing space in Sears. A brief look at the popularity of teen idols who sang such favorites as "Penny Loafers and Bobby Sox," "White Sport Coat and a Pink Carnation," "Pink Shoelaces," "Venus in Blue Jeans," and "Blue Suede Shoes," offers a profound indication of the burgeoning teenage population (think Archie and Veronica). Retailers were quick to cater to this brand new group of fad and fashion-conscious trendsetters with money to spend. Teens helped popularize coordinated sportswear, sweater sets, and jeans. In 1952 Vogue introduced "Young Idea," a feature aimed at seventeen to twenty-five year olds, while magazines such as *Seventeen* catered exclusively to this new market.

Little kids were quick to imitate the teen look. In 1959 they welcomed Barbie, the American teenage ideal, who was the first non-baby doll from Mattel. Children's apparel was no less smart than that of adults. In 1954 the *Ladies' Home Journal* noted: "Everybody looks young, feels young. Mothers are like big sisters in their shorts, pullovers and printed shirts."

From the New Look on, Paris continued to dominate high fashion as one silhouette followed another: A-line, H-line, chemise, trapeze, the hobble skirt, and high-waisted Directoire look. Buyers for American retail stores continued to make semi-annual forays to Paris to buy couture models which were given to manufacturers for the purpose of turning out mass-produced line-for-line copies of French designs, such as those by Monsieur X, whom everybody recognized instantly as Christian Dior. Perhaps the most significant influence on American fashion occurred when Gabrielle Chanel, the doyenne of prewar Paris fashion, reopened her house in 1954. In spite of a less than glowing reception by the press, her simple cardigan suit was welcomed by American women who understood the subtle luxury of style inherent in wearability and comfort. The "Chanel suit" soon became one of the most overworked phrases in fashion, and versions of it can be seen from the middle of the decade.

The most expensive fashions in Sears' pages, shown on the same high-fashion models photographed in *Vogue,* were somewhat toned-down versions of what was being featured on the runways of New York and Paris. Balenciaga's sack, Givenchy's chemise, and Yves Saint Laurent's trapeze were all available by mail or phone from Sears, but it is the simplicity of Chanel and her Seventh Avenue contemporaries, essentially based on sportswear, that pervades most of the clothing sold by Sears. Available from the catalog in every style and size range, including maternity separates, sportswear was America's forte. Women were leading rich and varied lives, requiring a broad range of garb, much of it sportswear, for many different occasions. Valerie Steele listed the wardrobe of a typical middle-income American woman as tabulated by an IBM machine at the U.S. exhibit in Moscow in 1959. It included a "winter weight long coat (fur-trimmed or untrimmed), one spring weight coat, one raincoat, five housedress type dresses, four afternoon 'dressy' type dresses, three suits, three skirts, six blouses, three sweaters, six slips, two petticoats, five nightgowns, eight pairs of panties, five brassieres, two corsets or girdles, two robes, six pairs of nylon stockings, two pairs of sport type socks, three pairs of dress gloves, one bathing suit, three pairs of play shorts, one pair of slacks and one play suit as well as accessories." Although the numbers were somewhat inflated for the benefit of the Soviet audience, the range is indicative of the lives American women were leading and the broad scope of their daily activities as well as their leisure.

Accessories included "seven pairs of shoes, four handbags, a dozen pieces of costume jewelry, four hats, and assorted scarves, belts, and other addenda." Notice the models in Sears—they wear hats with just about everything until the end of the decade, when juniors lead the way in hatlessness. Nor was an outfit complete without gloves appropriate to the occasion. Even Claire McCardell, the quintessentially American designer of modern clothing, extolled the virtues of hats and gloves:

Once upon a time you had to wear a hat. You don't have to today, but suddenly you may realize that your hair can't live up to all kinds of wind and weather. A hat should really be a hat. Ladylike. With great dignity and charm and distinction. . . .

A woman without gloves is a marked woman. It's like going barefoot to be without them. Gloves are traditionally a sign of dignity. . . . Everyone needs a good glove collection: short, long, glacé, doeskin, pigskin, cotton. . . . And Grandma's words of wisdom, 'A lady is known by her shoes and gloves,' still holds.

If this statement conjures up an image of Grace Kelly, it is not far from the mark. Her ladylike demeanor swept Prince Rainier of Monaco off his feet and they were wed with fairytale splendor to international fanfare in 1956.

The elegant, full-skirted dresses worn on and off-screen by the future princess were made of sumptuous, rigid fabrics. Brett Harvey, author of a women's history of the fifties was asked by a friend, "Did you ever think about the fact that all the fabrics we wore were stiff?" She remembered instantly: faille, taffeta, felt, piqué, stiffened nylon petticoats—everything was crisp, nothing was allowed to drape or cling.

Sportswear relied heavily on the new synthetics with Orlon and Acrilan sweaters, Orlon and wool-blend skirts in plaids or the ubiquitous Donegal, or salt-and-pepper, tweed for both sexes. Aside from denim for jeans and work clothes, corduroy appears to have been the fabric of choice for children's play clothes (sometimes warmed with linings of plaid flannel), men's sport jackets or slacks, and for just about every article of clothing made for girls and women including jumpers, skirts, shirts, long and short pants, and outerwear. The Ivy-league look was the hallmark of sportswear throughout the latter years of the decade. Every skirt, pair of shorts, or slacks boasted a cloth tab and back buckle, while button-down collars, penny loafers, and Bermuda shorts were favored by both sexes. The early fifties square-shouldered, double-breasted man's suit with draped trousers bowed to the Brooks Brothers "natural shoulder" single-breasted "Ivy league" style worn off campus as well as on. The beginnings of a youth rebellion could be seen in the popularity of black leather motorcycle jackets, immortalized on film by Marlon Brando in *The Wild One*. Winter coats sported cozy Orlon pile linings and many a raccoon was reborn as a collar, not to mention a coonskin cap like the one worn by Davy Crockett, aka Fess Parker, TV's "King of the Wild Frontier."

Special occasion clothing, long an American institution, included a new spring outfit every year for the entire family. Doubtless, every town had its version of the after-church Easter parade when new spring finery was displayed. Tradition required light-colored or navy blue suits for everybody, topped with straw hats for mom and the girls.

Sears understood America, and the catalog, described by David L. Cohn in *The Good Old Days, a History of Sears*, reflected the:

> tastes, wants, and desires not of a few wealthy women in the cities, but of millions of simple women living in the small towns and on the farms of America. . . . things in the catalog are the things people want. . . .
>
> The catalog is based purely upon public acceptance of the goods it offers, and not until the public has clearly signified that it wants a thing does that thing appear in its pages. We know, therefore, beyond all doubt, that the catalog's pictures of American life are drawn not from the imagination, but from the living model.

In 1955, due in no small measure to mass production and popular-priced retailers like Sears, the fashion industry ranked third in size in the United States. Sears' catalogs provided an accurate depiction of the healthy state of the country's economy and the lifestyle it afforded. In a 1955 address to the Fashion Group, Dorothy Shaver, the forward-thinking president of Lord & Taylor, first retailer to promote America's designers, echoed the words of Anatole France when she declared that American clothing has a "quality, an air, a spirit which is inescapable. It is implicit in the style, the fabric, the workmanship, yet it is something which transcends them all. They are the expression of a particular way of life, the expression of a free people, a happy people, a prosperous people, a young people. They are more descriptive of American production methods than a dozen lectures on economics or technology."

She might well have had Sears in mind when she continued, "To the rest of the civilized world, American fashions are a symbol of our democracy, proof that here one need not be rich to be well dressed, proof that in our land human values come before all others, proof that from the diversity of cultures from which America grew, a spirit of both equality and independence has arisen which is uniquely ours and new in the world." She credited American designers, manufacturers, and retailers for this special quality, which "explodes all theories that good taste must be exclusive and expensive. They have demonstrated in dollars and cents that objects in good taste can be successfully mass-produced and successfully mass-marketed. The proof of this is everywhere in America, in every city and every village, in every home and every office. For American women, at every income level, are the best dressed in the world."

JoAnne Olian
Sands Point, New York

Sanforized

Beautifully tailored
KERRYBROOKE CLASSIC

Cord-striped or
solid color cotton
with all these features

- Sanforized cotton is washable and will not shrink more than 1%
- Tape binding gives extra strength at waistline and armholes
- Self-covered triangular shoulder pads on snaps, easily removed to make washing and ironing easy
- Snap tapes at shoulders keep your lingerie straps from slipping down
- Concealed buttons firmly sewed, closely set to avoid gapping
- Belt is plastic in harmonizing color, won't peel or crack
- Hem two inches deep to give ample allowance for lengthening

5^{38}

The Buttoned Fly-front is an all-time fashion

This wonderful fly-front classic has everything . . good looks, fine tailoring, complete comfort. It is so useful for countless occasions, so becoming, that most customers who have worn it come back for more. The buttons all the way down are concealed by smart fly front. Buttons also on sleeves and pocket tabs. Made entirely to our specifications, and neat as a pin. *Sizes 12, 14, 16, 18, 20. Please state size.* See size chart on page 115. Shipping weight 1 pound.

Four Solid Pastels		*Four Colors in Stripes*	
027 D 7120—Pink	$5.38	027 D 7116—Red and white	$5.38
027 D 7121—Aqua green	5.38	027 D 7117—Blue and white	5.38
027 D 7122—Lavender	5.38	027 D 7118—Brown and white	5.38
027 D 7123—Gray	5.38	027 D 7119—Green and white	5.38

Sanforized
DENIM DUNGAREES

Sturdy 6-oz. or extra strong 8 oz. weight

With all the famous Kerrybrooke quality

Copper Rivets
at each corner of pockets to prevent ripping. Waistband button held firmly by copper rivet

Back Yoke
for firm fit and becoming lines. Big pocket below yoke. Both double-needle stitched

Zipper Placket
Smooth zipper placket at side is added value and gives firm, snug fit at hipline

Strong Seams
Double-needle stitching in bright color adds strength at pockets, waist, inside leg seam.

Sanforized for permanent fit. Denim guaranteed not to shrink more than 1%

5 belt loops bar-tacked to stand a lot of stress and strain without ripping

Contrasting thread stitch-ing adds to good looks, shows up fine tailoring

NOW ONLY
1^{74}
in 6-ounce denim
firm, sturdy, flexible

NOW ONLY
1^{94}
in 8-ounce denim
extra strong and durable

You certainly get a whale of a lot for your money when you order Sears famous Kerry-brooke dungarees. You get good tailoring, the smart, snug fit that's right for dun-garees, real comfort for general knock-about wear. They're durable as all get out, too. Wash separately. *Sizes 10, 12, 14, 16, 18, 20; see size chart, page 115. Please state correct size when you order.*

In 6-ounce Denim. Shpg. wt. 1 lb.
7 D 973—Navy blue   7 D 969—Barn red
7 D 970—Faded blue   Each........$1.74
In 8-ounce Denim. Shpg. wt. 1 lb. 3 oz.
7 D 949—Navy blue...............$1.94

F $1.98
Natural tan with
red or green trim

G $2.98
Red, green,
multicolor,
golden wheat
or white

Airily open as sandals

should be, yet

sturdily made the

Kerrybrooke way of

good quality leather

for lasting comfort ..

5 styles, under $3.00

Barefoot Sandals

Fun-loving feet take to carefree,

mint-cool flats like a duck takes to water

F Mexican-made, hand-woven Huaraches in natural tan leather, highlighted with red or green. Removable thong strap ties in front. Leather sole, flat leather heel.
• C (medium wide) in sizes 3, 4, 5, 6, 7, 8, 9. No half sizes. *Please state size.* Shpg. wt. 1 lb. 2 oz. See "How to Order" below.
54 D 7067—Natural tan, red trim . . . . Pair $1.98
54 D 7068—Natural tan, green trim . . . . . . Pair 1.98

H Sears lowest-priced genuine leather play shoe. Mexican-made, hand-woven huarache, sturdy and strong for hard wear. Leather insole, midsole, outsole and heel.
• C (medium wide) in sizes 3, 4, 5, 6, 7, 8, 9. No half sizes. *Please state size.* Shpg. wt. 1 lb. 2 oz. See "How to Order" below.
54 D 7196—Natural leather . . . . Pair $1.79

HOW TO ORDER HUARACHES: If you wear B or C width shoes, order your regular shoe size. For half size shoe, order huaraches half size smaller. *Example:* if you wear 5 or 5½, order Huaraches in 5.

K Choose it in white with covered or open back; in brown with covered back. Supple leather twin-strap flattie, nice with slacks or play clothes. Adjustable buckles to hold it firmly on your foot. Leather extension sole, ¾-inch heel.
• C (medium wide) 4½, 5, 5½, 6, 6½, 7, 7½, 8, 8½, 9. State size. Shpg. wt. 1 lb. 2 oz.
54 D 7152—White, closed back . . . . Pair $2.98
54 D 7151—Brown, closed back . . . . Pair 2.98
54 D 7153—White, open back . . . . Pair 2.98

G Cool as a cucumber. Colorful T-strap open leather sandal, all strips and straps. Pert pointed back. California-style platform, low wedge heel, composition sole.
• C (medium wide) 4½, 5, 5½, 6, 6½, 7, 7½, 8, 8½, 9. State size. Shpg. wt. 1 lb. 2 oz.
54 D 7475—Red leather . . . . Pair $2.98
54 D 7474—Green leather . . . . Pair 2.98
54 D 7476—Multicolor leather . . . . Pair 2.98
54 D 7477—White leather . . . . Pair 2.98
54 D 7473—Golden Wheat . . . . Pair 2.98

J Lovely new supple leather sling pump with open sabot strap. V-line vamp, cushion platform, wedge heel, leather sole. Rich two-color combinations; plain colors.
• AA (narrow) 5, 5½, 6, 6½, 7, 7½, 8, 8½, 9.
• B (medium) 4½, 5, 5½, 6, 6½, 7, 7½, 8, 8½, 9. *State size, width.* Shpg. wt. 1 lb. 2 oz.
◆54 D 7123Y—White, brown trim . . . . Pair $4.98
◆54 D 7122Y—Golden wheat, brown . . . . . Pair 4.98
◆54 D 7120Y—Red ◆54 D 7121Y—Green . . Pair 4.98

L Gypsy colors that look so pretty with summer whites and prints. Criss cross straps to give your feet a slender look. Smooth leather; curved covered back. Plump platform, low wedge heel, rubber sole.
• B (medium) 4½, 5, 5½, 6, 6½, 7, 7½, 8, 8½, 9. *State size.* Shpg. wt. 1 lb. 2 oz.
54 D 7479—Multicolor . . . Pair $1.98
54 D 7481—Golden wheat . Pair 1.98
54 D 7480—Tangerine . . . Pair 1.98
54 D 7482—White . . . . . . Pair 1.98

H $1.79

J $4.98
Golden wheat
or white with
brown trim,
red or green

K $2.98
White or brown with
covered back, also
white with open back

L $1.98
Multicolor,
golden wheat,
tangerine
or white

SEARS OWN KERRYBROOKE WEEKENDER

Four-piece Sanforized cotton wardrobe

at a price you'd pay for one smart outfit

- Twin dots in fresh, smart navy and white
- Each piece is an outstanding fashion
- They combine to make 4 stunning outfit
- Glamorous for dress, street or playtime
- Sears dreamed it up—only Sears has i

4 pieces complete in a new dotted package $6.97

The Skirt is navy blue Sanforized cotton with white polka dots. It's gathered full all around with wide waistband, zipper placket. The Riviera Shirt is a 4-star fashion by itself, and you'll wear it with many other things. The Bra is neat as a pin, double fabric, ties in back (Bra and Riviera shirt are white with navy dots). The Shorts combine both twin dots, have a zipper placket, cuffed, hems. All parts washable, with max. fab. shrink. 1%. Sizes 10, 12, 14, 16, 18; see size chart, page 115. Please state size. Shipping weight complete, 1 lb. 14 oz.
07 D 692—Navy blue and white complete 4-piece outfit.......................$6.97

IMPORTANT CUSTOMER INFORMATION
Catalog numbers beginning with "0" shipped from Philadelphia or Kansas City. Order and pay postage only from Sears nearest mail order house. Other numbers shipped from nearest mail order house.

GAY SHORTS

Sanforized Cottons firm weave, firmly stitched, and they won't shrink over 1%

[A] VAGABOND SHORTS, cotton twill. High waistline split and curved in front. Contrasting shoestring belt. Cuff finish at hems. Zips at center back. Washable. Sizes 10, 12, 14, 16, 18. State size. Shipping weight 8 oz.
7 D 477—Yellow.....$1.89
7 D 478—White..... 1.89
7 D 479—Navy blue. 1.89

[A] $1.89

[B] PINCHECK DENIM, button trimmed tab in front. Zipper placket. Cuff finish hems. Wash separately. Sizes 10, 12, 14, 16, 18. Please state size. Shipping weight 8 oz.
7 D 481—Green.....$1.69
7 D 482—Med. blue.. 1.69
7 D 483—Red...... 1.69

[B] $1.69

[C] LIGHT OR DARK cotton twill shorts with button tab in front. Zipper placket. Cuff hems. Washable. Sizes 10, 12, 14, 16, 18. State size. Shipping weight 5 oz.
7 D 489—White.....$1.59
7 D 490—Yellow..... 1.59
7 D 491—Navy blue. 1.59

[C] $1.59

[D] TATTERSALL CHECK cotton twill, button tab in front. Cuff edges. Zipper placket. Washable. Sizes 10, 12, 14, 16, 18. State size. Shpg. wt. 7 oz.
7 D 480—White with red and navy blue......$1.69

[D] $1.69

[E] DENIM BOXER SHORTS with elastic waistband. Wash separately. Sizes 10, 12, 14, 16, 18. State size. Shpg. wt. 7 oz.
7 D 484—Yellow.......97c
7 D 485—Navy blue....97c
7 D 486—Red........97c

[E] 97c

[F] STITCH TRIMMED heavy weight, extra fine cotton gabardine. Two big pockets. Zipper in back, cuff hems. Washable. Sizes 10, 12, 14, 16, 18. State size. Shipping weight 10 oz.
7 D 487—Navy with white
7 D 488—White with navy
Each..............$2.39

[F] $2.39

FOR MISSES

B $7.49

C $7.49
Also Size 38 to 42

D $6.98

E $5.98

A $6.49

WRINKLE-RESISTANT JERSEY..

fine, smooth rayon that holds pleats beautifully .. rarely needs pressing

[A] Cool, young looking .. eyelets and fine woven mesh design in black, black plastic belt and buttons. Unpressed pleats all around the skirt. Dry cleaning recommended. *Sizes 12, 14, 16, 18, 20. See size charts, page 115. Shpg. wt. 1 lb. 8 oz.*
031 D 8415—White   031 D 8416—Aqua blue
031 D 8417—Medium pink   *State size* ...... Each $6.49

[B] Smooth and smart looking. Pleats all around the skirt, shining gold-color metal buttons. Can be hand washed separately; dry cleaning recommended. *Sizes 12, 14, 16, 18, 20. See size charts, page 115. Measure; state correct size.*
031 D 8412—Black   031 D 8413—Medium pink
031 D 8414—Aqua blue   Shpg. wt. 1 lb. 8 oz..Each $7.49

[C] Flattering and wonderfully practical. Yoke and pleats all around the skirt; draped pockets. Can be hand washed separately; dry cleaning recommended. Size charts, page 115. *Sizes 12, 14, 16, 18, 20; also 38, 40, 42. Shpg. wt. 1 lb. 8 oz.*
031 D 8418—Black and white checks. *State size* $7.49
031 D 8419—Navy blue and white checks. *State size* 7.49

CRISP, FINELY RIBBED RAYON..

wrinkle-resistant, easy to wash and iron .. comes in rich, muted colors

[D] Fly-front with beautiful details .. convertible collar, front shoulder yoke, patch pockets, 5-gore skirt, finely stitched collar, cuffs, fly front. Hand wash separately. Leather-like belt. *Sizes 12, 14, 16, 18, 20. Shpg. wt. 1 lb. 8 oz.*
031 D 8421—Dusty rose   031 D 8422—Powder blue
031 D 8423—Aqua green   *State size* .... Each $6.98

[E] Flattering two-tone dress in deep colors with lighter shade inset on the front of the bodice and the 4-gore bias skirt. Expertly tailored. Hand wash separately. *Sizes 12, 14, 16, 18, 20. Measure; state correct size. Shpg. wt. 1 lb. 8 oz.*
031 D 8424—Bright navy blue with light powder blue ..$5.98
031 D 8425—Bright navy blue with dusty rose 5.98
031 D 8426—Black with gray 5.98

Please order your correct size. You'll look smarter and save unnecessary alterations. Follow measuring instructions carefully and check with size charts on page 115. Numbers beginning with "0" are shipped from Philadelphia or Kansas City. Order and pay postage from Sears nearest mail order house.

OUR BEST KERRYBROOKE Dresses, Shown on these 2 Pages, are Expertly Cut ..

1. 2-inch hem for easy lengthening .. except on bias and very full skirts which require narrow taped hems for proper drape.
2. ⅞-inch side seams on slim skirts, so you can adjust the fit. Smaller seams on full and bias skirts, which are self adjusting.
3. Neat zipper placket .. can't gap, saves time.
4. Reinforced belt that keeps its shape.

Kerrybrooke
THE RIGHT WAY
TO SAY
FASHIONS

$8.49
Juniors' sizes only

$5.98

$6.49

$5.98
Sanforized

$6.98

Cottons .. MADE BETTER 8 WAYS (see below)

COMBED YARN DOTTED SWISS .. very fine and sheer with applied white dots (guaranteed permanent) and permanent-finish white organdy. Grosgrain ribbon run through slots on collar and around full skirt .. bright red ribbon on navy, dark brown on aqua. Remove ribbon; hand wash dress separately. *Sizes 9, 11, 13, 15, 17.* Size charts on page 115. *Please be sure to state size wanted.* Shipping weight 2 pounds.

031D8152—Navy blue.. $8.49
031D8153—Aqua green. 8.49

WAFFLE PIQUE .. very fine quality in a wonderful new print .. washes beautifully, keeps its color. Zipper front, fabric ties on the sleeves, corded belt, full gathered skirt all around. Washable. *Sizes 9, 11, 13, 15, 17; also 10, 12, 14, 16, 18. Please measure carefully; state correct size.* Shipping weight 1 lb. 8 oz.

031D8155—White with aqua blue and dark brown.. $5.98
031D8156—White with rose and navy blue........$5.98
031D8157—White with lime green and black......$5.98

WASHFAST PIQUE .. superior quality with very fine rib .. won't shrink more than 1½% .. white grounds with aqua, yellow or green dots outlined in navy blue. Pretty off-shoulder collar with loops all around .. elastic at sides to hold it comfortably and securely. Full 4-gore bias skirt. *Sizes 9, 11, 13, 15, 17; also 10, 12, 14, 16, 18.* Size charts, page 115. *Measure; state size.* Shpg. wt. 2 lbs.

031D8158—Aqua blue.. $6.49
031D8159—Yellow..... 6.49
031D8160—Bright green 6.49

COMBED YARN GINGHAM .. washfast, woven checks .. won't shrink more than 1%. Bow-tie collar, cuffs and inset bands around full skirt are white eyelet embroidered pique. Front midriff with gathers above and at shoulders; half belt keeps waistline snug, ties in big bow in back. *Sizes 9, 11, 13, 15, 17; also 10, 12, 14, 16, 18. Measure; state size.* Shpg. wt. 1 lb. 8 oz.

031 D 8161—Red and white
031 D 8162—Medium blue and white......Each $5.98

WONDERFUL OUTFIT

for every special date

WASHFAST WAFFLE PIQUE .. superior quality that stays fresh and crisp. Smooth little jacket with matching plastic buttons.. pretty low-cut dress with heavy, dyed-to-match cotton lace all around the bodice, full 4-gore bias skirt .. bodice dips in back, back zipper. An adorable outfit for everything from beach parties to proms. *Sizes 9, 11, 13, 15, 17; also 10, 12, 14, 16, 18.* Measure; check with size charts .. see page 115. *State your correct size.* Shpg. wt. 2 lbs.

031 D 8164—White........$6.98
031 D 8165—Petal pink..... 6.98
031 D 8166—Light blue..... 6.98

MADE BETTER 8 WAYS to Look Smarter, Fit Better, Wear Longer

5. All hems are blind stitched .. all seams (except armholes) are pinked .. side seams are pressed open.

6. Waist, shoulder and yoke seams are taped or double stitched to retain style and good lines.

7. New type shoulder pads..well made, neatly tacked, easy to remove.

8. Buttons are sewn separately and securely .. buttonholes are well made.

THRIFTY COOL COTTONS for little girls .. sizes 3 to 6x

$1.09

Pique cotton sun dress. Contrasting piping on skirt, bodice ruffle. Strap tie at shoulder. Washable. *Sizes 3, 4, 5, 6, 6x.* See size chart, page 9. *State size.* Shipping weight 7 ounces.
29 D 1100—Yellow
29 D 1101—Pink
Each............$1.09

$1.29

Multicolor floral print on 80-sq. percale. Ruffle at yoke, bottom of skirt. Button back to waist. Tie back sash. Washable. *Sizes 3, 4, 5, 6, 6x.* Size chart, page 9. *State size.* Shipping weight 6 ounces.
29 D 1102—Blue print
Each............$1.29

$1.29

Permanent finish organdy . . . lace ruffle yoke and skirt flounce. Back sash. Button back. Hand washable. *Sizes 3, 4, 5, 6, 6x.* Size chart, page 9. *State size.* Shipping weight 4 ounces.
29 D 1103—Pink
29 D 1104—Blue
Each............$1.29

"WALT DISNEY"
Movie and Cartoon Stars

in bright colors on sturdy, cotton playwear .. made for fun and comfort. Sizes 2 to 6x.

[A] NAVY BLUE DENIM BOXER SHORTS with fun-loving Mickey and Minnie Mouse frolicking on the front. Elastic shirring all around. Back patch pocket. Sanforized—won't shrink over 1%. Wash separately. *Sizes 2, 3, 4, 5, 6, 6x.* Size chart page 9. *State size.* Shpg. wt. 6 oz.
29 D 4505—Navy blue...........$1.19

[B] DENIM BOXER LONGIES. Donald Duck and Family printed on front. Elastic shirred waist. Back patch pocket. Sanforized, won't shrink over 1%. Wash separately. *Sizes 2, 3, 4, 5, 6, 6x.* Size chart, page 9. *State size.* Shpg. wt. 8 oz.
29 D 4328—Navy blue...........$1.59

[C] DENIM OVERALLS. Mickey and Minnie and the rest of the family colorfully printed on front. Self lined bib. Button-on suspenders. Back patch pocket. Sanforized, won't shrink over 1%. Wash separately. *Sizes 2, 3, 4, 5, 6, 6x.* Size chart, page 9. *State size.* Shpg. wt. 9 oz.
29 D 4207—Navy blue...........$1.89

[D] COMBED COTTON POLO SHIRT with Mickey Mouse cowboy print on front. Ribbed knit crew neck. Washable. *Sizes 3, 4, 6.* See size chart on page 9. *Please state size.* Shipping weight 4 ounces.
29 D 4732—Yellow..Ea. 98c 2 for $1.92
29 D 4733—White..Ea. 98c 2 for $1.92

GAILY RUFFLED SUN SUITS

$1.14

Washable 80-sq. percale. Ruffles on bib and back. Elastic back. Button-on suspenders. *Sizes 3, 4, 5, 6, 6x.* See size chart, page 9. *State size.* Shpg. wt. 5 oz.
29 D 4543—Multicolor plaid...........$1.14

$1.98

Washfast, Sanforized cotton broadcloth. Attached pants. Max. shrinkage 1%. *Sizes 3, 4, 5, 6, 6x.* Size chart, page 9. *State size.* Wt. 7 oz.
29 D 4544—Blue, pink
29 D 4545—Yellow, aqua green..Suit $1.98

Shirt and Shorts

$1.98 Set

Plaid gingham shirt; chambray shorts. Washable, Sanforized—won't shrink over 1%. *Sizes 3, 4, 5, 6, 6x.* See size chart, page 9. *State size.* Shipping weight 8 ounces.
29 D 4546—Plaid shirt, aqua green shorts. $1.98

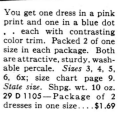

WASHABLE PERCALES
2 FOR $1.69

You get one dress in a pink print and one in a blue dot .. each with contrasting color trim. Packed 2 of one size in each package. Both are attractive, sturdy, washable percale. *Sizes 3, 4, 5, 6, 6x;* size chart page 9. *State size.* Shpg. wt. 10 oz.
29 D 1105—Package of 2 dresses in one size....$1.69

$3.79

$3.79

BOYVILLE JR. LONGIES . . Sanforized cottons, washfast rayon

$1.44 $1.88 $1.69 $2.69

Medium weight **$1.44** cotton twill, Sanforized (fab. shrinkage 1%). Self-lined bib, waist. Buckle suspenders. Side openings. Fly opening. Wash separately. *State size* 3, 4, 5, 6, 7, 8, 9, 10. Size chart, page 76. Shpg. wt. 1 lb. 3 oz.
40D5608—Cadet blue
40D5609—Dk.brown$1.44

Vat-dyed Glen **$1.88** plaid on Sanforized cotton twill (fab. shrinkage 1%). Zip fly, pleats, 3 pockets. Button-on suspenders, belt loops, cuffs. Washable. Shpg. wt. 1 lb. 4 oz. *State size* 3, 4, 5, 6, 7, 8, 9, 10. Size chart, page 76.
40 D 5711—Blue plaid
40 D 5712—Brown . . $1.88

Solid color San- **$1.69** forized cotton twill (shrinkage 1%). Button fly, button-on suspenders. 3 pockets, pleats. Wash separately. Regular money-back guarantee! Shpg. wt. 1 lb. 4 oz. *State size* 3, 4, 5, 6, 7, 8, 9, 10. Size chart, page 76.
40 D 5715—Dark brown
40 D 5716—Navy. . . . $1.69

Cool rayon, **$2.69** GUARANTEED WASHFAST Suspender Longies. Permanent shrinkage control (fabric shrinkage 2%). Sunfast. Zip fly, 3 pockets, pleats, cuffs. Shpg. wt. 1 lb. 4 oz. *State size* 3, 4, 5, 6, 7, 8, 9, 10. See size chart on page 76.
40 D 3231—Blue
40 D 3232—Brown. . $2.69

WESTERN PLAY OUTFITS

Boys', Girls' sizes 4-12 **$3.79** Ea.

9-PC. RANCHER SET. Leopard-printed cotton vest, chaps. Cotton flannel shirt. Belt, holster. Toy pistol, cotton hat, bandanna, lariat. *State size* 4, 6, 8, 10, 12. Size chart, page 76.
40 D 4551—9-pc. set. Shpg. wt. 2 lbs. 2 oz. . $3.79

8-PC. COWGIRL SET. Leopard-printed cotton skirt, vest. Cotton plaid blouse. Genuine leather belt, holster. Cotton hat, lariat, toy pistol. *Sizes* 4, 6, 8, 10, 12. Size chart, page 76.
40 D 4547—8-pc. set. Shpg. wt. 1 lb. 13 oz. . $3.79

BASEBALL SUITS

at slashed prices!

Economy **$1.89**

[C] 6-PC. UNIFORM. Gray cotton flannel. Short sleeve *shirt*. Matching *pants*; hip pocket. Imitation leather *belt*. Cotton flannel *cap*. Complete felt *alphabet* for team name. Footless cotton *sox*. Shpg. wt. 1 lb. 13 oz. *State size* 4, 6, 8, 10, 12, 14. See size chart on page 76.
40 D 4527—6-pcs.
Was $2.79 . . . . $1.89

Our finest **$2.89**

[D] Boyville Jr. finest 6-pc. outfit. Better grade gray sueded cotton; short sleeve shirt. Pants have belt loops, hip pocket. Black felted cap. Cotton footless sox. Leather belt. Complete felt alphabet for team name. Sears money-back guarantee! Shpg. wt. 1 lb. 14 oz. *State size* 4, 6, 8, 10, 12, 14, 16. See size chart on page 76.
40 D 4529—6-pc. set
Was $4.49 . . . . $2.89

Roy Rogers Dale Evans

Each Set **$4.88**

[A] ROY ROGERS 8-PIECE COWBOY SET. Cotton twill chaps. 2-tone Sanforized cotton shirt; cotton hat, bandanna. Leather belt, holster, lariat, toy pistol. Shpg. wt. 2 lbs. 2 oz. Sizes 4, 6, 8, 10, 12. Chart, pg. 76.
40D4533—Cowboy Set $4.88

[B] DALE EVANS (MRS. ROY ROGERS) 8-PC. SET. Cotton twill skirt. Matching vest. Sanforized two-tone cotton (max. shrinkage 1%) blouse. Hat, leather belt, holster. Toy pistol, lariat. Sizes, weight above.
40D4534—Cowgirl Set $4.88

$4.88

$1.89 $2.89

$4.88

Newest, most flattering

DRESS OF 1951

The new tapering silhouette . . . . slim skirt with peg pocket effect, front shirring, 3-gore back. The new plunging neckline to wear modestly or glamorously low. Set-in sleeves with side shirring; shiny plastic belt. Expertly cut, made better 8 ways

$8.98 Each

Your choice of 3 of our finest fabrics
In Misses' and Shorter Women's Sizes

A POLKA DOTS on very smooth rayon crepe that drapes as gracefully and feels as soft as silk. Dry clean. Shpg. wt. 1 lb. 8 oz.
Sizes 12, 14, 16, 18 and 20.
Measure; state size.
031 K 8512—Navy blue with white polka dots. $8.98

Sizes 16½, 18½, 20½, 22½, 24½. Measure; state size.
031 K 8712—Navy blue with white polka dots. $8.98

B ROSE-IN-BLOOM PRINT on white backgrounds . . rayon jersey of extra fine quality that resists wrinkles. Dry clean. Shpg. wt. 1 lb. 8 oz.
Sizes 12, 14, 16, 18, 20.
031 K 9509—Pink, brown, green print
031 K 9510—Lilac, black, gold print
031 K 9511—Fuchsia, violet, turquoise

Sizes 16½, 18½, 20½, 22½, 24½.
031 K 9809—Pink, brown, green print
031 K 9810—Lilac, black, gold print
031 K 9811—Fuchsia, violet, turquoise
Measure; state size. . . . . . . Each $8.98

C SOLID COLORS in very finely ribbed rayon that looks and feels like rich, heavy silk . . famous as "our most beautiful crepe." Dry clean. State size. Shpg. wt. 1 lb. 8 oz.
Sizes 12, 14, 16, 18, 20.
031 K 8509—Navy blue $8.98
031 K 8510—Black. 8.98

Sizes 16½, 18½, 20½, 22½, 24½. Measure; state size.
031 K 8709—Navy blue $8.98
031 K 8710—Black. 8.98

Costume Drama

High platforms, high heels . .

To star you as a leading lady . . wherever you go

Fashion-favored high lustre calf or patent;

suede, in lush colors . . Kerrybrookes, their

fine fit, fine quality guaranteed

[N] Superbly beautiful bracelet sandal for dining, dancing hours; soaring high on a ½-inch platform and slender 3-inch heels. Polished calfskin that endures in your affections as it does in your wardrobe, or whisper-soft suede. A slim strap spotlights your dainty ankle, adjusts for a firm fit. Our finest quality construction, glove-fitting, flexible. Leather lined and soled.
• A (medium narrow) width in sizes 5½, 6, 6½, 7, 7½, 8, 8½, 9.
• C (medium wide) width in sizes 4, 4½, 5, 5½, 6, 6½, 7, 7½, 8, 8½ and 9. *Please state size and width.* Shpg. wt. 1 lb. 2 oz.

054 D 8519—Black calfskin . . . . .Pair $7.95
054 D 8523—Blue calfskin . . . . .Pair 7.95
054 D 8520—Golden wheat color suede .Pair 7.95
054 D 8522—Gray suede . . . . .Pair 7.95

[P] Exquisite sling pump, open vamp, ¼-inch platform, 2¾-inch heel, leather sole. Finest Kerrybrooke quality.
• AA (narrow) sizes 5½ to 9.
• B (medium) sizes 4 to 9.
Half sizes too. *Please state size.* Shipping weight 1 lb. 2 oz.

♦ 54 D 8547Y—Black patent
♦ 54 D 8548Y—Blue calfskin
♦ 54 D 8549Y—Cognac (brown) calf
♦ 54 D 8550Y—White suede.Pr. $6.98

[R] Siren bracelet sandal to dance away your happiest hours. V-throat, lacey vamp openings. ½-inch platform, 3-inch heels, leather sole.
• B (medium) sizes 4½ to 9.
Half sizes too. *Please state size.* Shipping weight 1 lb. 2 oz.

♦ 54 D 8533Y—Black patent.Pr. $6.98
♦ 54 D 8534Y—Red calfskin . Pr. 6.98
♦ 54 D 8535Y—Green calf . .Pr. 6.98
♦ 54 D 8532Y—Blue calf . . .Pr. 6.98

[T] Fascinating sling pump. Flattering curved throat. ⅜-inch platform; slender 3-in. heel, leather sole. 4 colors.
• A (medium narrow) 5½ to 9.
• C (medium wide) in 4 to 9.
Half sizes too. *State size, width.* Shpg. wt. 1 lb. 2 oz.
054 D 8489—Green calf
054 D 8487—Golden wheat calf
054 D 8492—Black patent
054 D 8491—Blue calf . . . .Pair $7.95

[V] Soft suede, bright patent, or smooth leather pump. Tiny vamp openings to flatter pretty feet. ¼-inch platform, 2¼-inch heel, leather sole. Wear it with party finery.
• C (medium wide) 4½ to 9.
Half sizes too. *Please state size.* Shipping weight 1 lb. 2 oz.

♦ 54 D 8539Y—White suede.Pr. $5.98
♦ 54 D 8536Y—Black patent.Pr. 5.98
♦ 54 D 8537Y—Blue leather.Pr. 5.98

[W] For those special dates, a sweet bracelet sandal that flatters your foot in a lady-like way. ⅜-inch platform to make the high 2⅜-inch heel feel lower. Leather sole.
• B (medium) sizes 4½ to 9.
Half sizes too. *Please state size.* Shipping weight 1 lb. 2 oz.

♦ 54 D 8540Y—Black calf . .Pr. $6.98
♦ 54 D 8542Y—White suede.Pr. 6.98
♦ 54 D 8541Y—Blue calf . . . .Pr. 6.98

[X] Graceful accent for smart suits. Curved straps make little of your feet. Openly cool; perched comfortably high on a ¼-inch platform, 2½-inch heel. Leather sole.
• A (medium narrow) 5½ to 9.
• C (medium wide) in 4 to 9.
Half sizes too. *State size, width.* Shpg. wt. 1 lb. 2 oz.
054 D 8524—Black patent . Pair $7.95
054 D 8525—Blue calf . . . Pair 7.95

Catalog numbers beginning with 054 mean Kansas City and Minneapolis orders sent from Chicago. ♦ Numbers mean Minneapolis orders are shipped from Chicago. Order and pay postage from your nearest Sears mail order house.

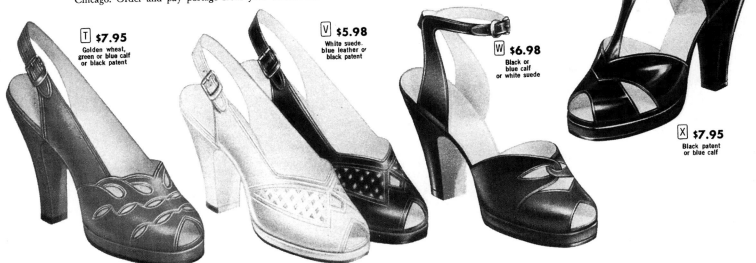

[N] $7.95
Black or blue calf;
golden wheat or gray suede

[P] $6.98
Black patent,
blue or brown
calf, white suede

[R] $6.98
Black patent,
red, green or
blue calf

[T] $7.95
Golden wheat,
green or blue calf
or black patent

[V] $5.98
White suede,
blue leather or
black patent

[W] $6.98
Black or
blue calf
or white suede

[X] $7.95
Black patent
or blue calf

$153.30 cash Tax included

$167.40 cash Tax included

10 [1951]

FUR SCARFS TO TOP EVERYTHING

Fashionable furs in 3, 4, 5 skin arrangements

Sears prices are low for such fine quality

SABLE-DYED SQUIRREL
Each skin about 16 in. long
074 D 0636E—Brown
Set of 3 skins
Shpg. wt. 9 oz.....$17.10
074 D 0637E—Brown
Set of 4 skins
Shpg. wt. 12 oz.$22.80
074 D 0638E—Brown
Set of 5 skins
Shpg. wt. 15 oz.$28.50

SABLE-DYED KOLINSKY
Each skin about 18 in. long
074 D 0639E–Sable brown
Set of 3 skins
Shpg. wt. 9 oz.....$29.70
074 D 0640E–Sable brown
Set of 4 skins
Shpg. wt. 12 oz.$39.60
074 D 0641E–Sable brown
Set of 5 skins
Shpg. wt. 15 oz.$49.50

GENUINE MINK
Each skin about 23 in. long
074 D 0642E–Mink bro
Set of 3 skins
Shpg. wt. 9 oz.$54.00
074 D 0643E–Mink brown
Set of 4 skins
Shpg. wt. 12 oz.$72.00
074 D 0644E–Mink brown
Set of 5 skins
Shpg. wt. 15 oz.$90.00

5 skins illustrated

All fur prices include 20%
Federal Excise Tax.

Mink-dyed Marmot Cape

$15.50 down, $10.50 monthly, Easy Terms

Prime pelts with the rich look of real mink, with the fine styling of real mink. These are plump, glossy pelts skillfully fashioned into a cape of stunning beauty, with easy shoulders, smart collar and gracefully scalloped border. Rayon lined. Length about 26 in. *Misses' sizes* 10, 12, 14, 16, 18, 20. Measure; size chart on page 267. *Please state size.* Shipping weight 3 pounds.
074 D 0635E — Mink brown. Total cash price (includes 20% Federal Excise Tax)........$153.30

Genuine Natural Silver Fox Jacket

$17.00 down, $12 monthly on Easy Terms

Fashion and glamour for little money in this handsome fur with silver highlights. Choice skins, expertly worked to enhance the full, natural beauty of fur, especially in the clever collar-effect. Sleeves unsnap . . can be worn as cape or jacket. Rayon lining, undersleeves and sides. About 27 in. long. *Misses' sizes* 10, 12, 14, 16, 18, 20. Measure; see size chart, page 267. *State size.* Shpg. wt. 3 lbs.
074 D 0634E—Genuine Silver Fox. Total cash price (includes 20% Federal Excise Tax)........$167.40

$42.00 cash Tax included

$71.40 cash Tax included

$76.20 cash Tax included

Black Caracul-dyed Kidskin Cape

$4.50 down, $5 monthly on Easy Terms

Sleek, classic sling style with all the luster and swirl of expensive caracul. Dresses up suits, dresses, cloth coats beautifully. Well-styled shoulders; full swirling cut to allow for suits. Rayon lining. About 28 inches long. *Misses' sizes* 10, 12, 14, 16, 18, 20. Size chart, page 267. *State size.* Shpg. wt. 3 lbs.
074 D 0645E—Jet black. Total cash price (includes 20% Federal Excise Tax)..................$42.00

Popular Red Fox Jacket in 3 shades

$7.50 down, $6 monthly on Easy Terms

Sears low-priced. Rayon lining and undersleeves; armshields. Sling straps. Round collar-effect in back. About 26 in. long. *Misses' sizes* 10, 12, 14, 16, 18, 20. Size chart, page 267. *State size.* Shpg. wt. 3 lbs.
074 D 0646E—Dyed Norwegian blue
074 D 0647E—Dyed Paradise silver
074 D 0648E—Natural red
Total cash price (includes tax)........Each $71.40

Black-dyed African Kidskin Jacket

$8.00 down, $7.00 monthly on Easy Terms

Rich-looking, smooth, supple fur, beautifully lustrous . . masterfully worked into a top-fashion tuxedo front jacket with the new, soft, natural shoulders, deep armholes and wide sleeves with convertible cuffs. The full, flared pyramid back falls in graceful ripples to form a picture of fashion elegance. Rayon lined. Length about 27 in. *Misses' sizes* 10, 12, 14, 16, 18, 20. Size chart, page 267. *State size.*
074 D 0649E—Black. Shpg. wt. 3 lbs. Total cash price (includes 20% Federal Excise Tax).........$76.20

Dramatic Styles THAT ARE EASY-TO-WEAR

$3.98

TWIN-QUILL BONNET in smooth sisal straw has fashion's latest look with its glamour-accent of rayon velvet tubular band. Rayon veil. *State color* All navy blue or black. White with black. Toast tan with dark brown. Shpg. wt. 1 lb.
078 K 2130—Fits 21¾–22¼ in..$3.98
078 K 2131—Fits 22½–23¼ in.. 3.98

$2.59

DRESSY SHEER BRAID HELMET has fashion-smart rayon velvet covered buttons . . . an eye-catching frame for your face. Wired to fit head snugly. Rayon veil. *Please state color* All black or navy blue. White with black. White with navy blue. Shipping weight 12 ounces.
078 K 2145—Fits 21¾–22¼ in...$2.59

$3.98

RIPPLE-BRIM BONNET in straw-like cloth with dainty flowers and rayon velvet loops. Rayon veil. *State color* Beige or pink, blending flowers. Navy blue or black, white flowers. White, moss green trim; white flowers. Shipping wt. 1 lb.
078 K 2120—Fits 21¾–22¼ in...$3.98
078 K 2121—Fits 22½–23¼ in... 3.98

$3.59

THE BIG, BEAUTIFUL PICTURE HAT to make you picture-pretty. Sheer braid with rustling rayon taffeta band and backbow. *State color* All white, navy blue or black. Shipping wt. 1 lb. 15 oz.
078K2100—Fits 21¾–22¼ in..$3.59
078K2101—Fits 22½–23¼ in.. 3.59

$4.49

FLATTERING UPSWEPT BRIM accented with rich rayon velvet tubing. Straw braid. Rayon veil. *Colors* White with black trim. Wheat tan with light brown trim. All black or all navy blue. *State color.* Shipping weight 1 lb. 4 oz.
078K2115—Fits 21¾–22¼ in.$4.49
078K2116—Fits 22½–23¼ in. 4.49

$3.98

PROFILE STRAW BRAID banded with rayon velvet tubing. Bright novelty stick-up. Rayon veil. *State color* White with black, white flowers. Beige with dark brown, eggshell flowers. Navy or black, white flowers. Shipping wt. 1 lb.
078 K 2150—Fits 21¾–22¼ in...$3.98
078 K 2151—Fits 22½–23¼ in... 3.98

$3.29

SIDE-ACCENTED off-face hat of fine straw-braid. Grosgrain ribbon binding, band, and bow. Rayon veil. *Colors* Toast tan with dark brown trim. All white, navy blue or black. *State color.* Shipping weight 15 ounces.
078K2140—Fits 21¾–22¼ in..$3.29
078K2141—Fits 22½–23¼ in.. 3.29

$3.98

FLATTERING RAYON TAFFETA fan-loops and band . . fashion-rich accents on head-hugging beauty. Fine quality straw braid. *Please state color* All navy blue, black, or white. Wheat tan with light brown. Shipping weight 1 pound.
078 K 2125—Fits 21¾–22¼ in...$3.98
078 K 2126—Fits 22½–23¼ in... 3.98

$3.69

GLISTENING "CANDY" STRAW CLOCHE has striking rayon velvet "wings" and a draped sash-band. *Colors* Wheat tan, white or pink with black trim. All navy or all black. *State color wanted.* Shipping weight 14 oz.
078K2155—Fits 21¾–22¼ in..$3.69
078K2156—Fits 22½–23¼ in.. 3.69

$4.98

SIDE-SWEPT HAT in fine straw braid, softly draped for maximum flattery. Feather winged bird and rayon veiling. *State color* Black, navy blue with white. Wheat tan with dk. brown. Lt. gray. Shpg. wt. 1 lb. 1 oz.
078 K 2010—Fits 21¾–22¼ in...$4.98
078 K 2011—Fits 22½–23¼ in... 4.98
078 K 2012—Fits 23½–24¼ in... 4.98

$3.49

EXQUISITE FLORAL WREATH and rayon velvet accents on lustrous straw-like cloth. Rayon veil. Wonderful now-into-summer style. *State color* Beige with light brown. Navy blue or black with white. All pink or all white. Shpg. wt. 14 oz.
078 K 2135—Fits 21¾–22¼ in...$3.49
078 K 2136—Fits 22½–23¼ in... 3.49

$3.69

LUXURIOUS RAYON TAFFETA gathered into a striking off-face ruffle-trim. Smartly looped at the side, richly detailed crown. A glamorous accent to any outfit. *Colors* All black, dark brown, or navy blue. *State color.* Shpg. wt. 1 lb. 5 oz.
078 K 2105—Fits 21¾–22¼ in...$3.69
078 K 2106—Fits 22½–23¼ in... 3.69

Sharkskin Suits of Pure Wool Worsted

$44.50 Cash

Only $4.50 Down

Also larger sizes

A Stripe patterned Sharkskin

B Solid-tone Sharkskin

C Overplaid pattern Sharkskin

Gold Bond
THE RIGHT WAY
TO SAY
MEN'S SHOES

[F] [G] [H] [J]

Hand Paints

Hand-painted designs in colors that are bright and right! Soft rayon and rayon-and-nylon fabrics. Wool-lined. 4½ in. wide; 50 in. long (except [E], [F], [G], which are 48 to 49 in.). Drape-Stitch construction (in [A], [B], [C], [D]) makes it easy to tie a natural dimple knot. Shpg. wt. ea. 4 oz. Boxed.

[A] [B] [C] [D]	[E] [F] [G]
$1.47 Each	**97c** Each
Any **2** for **$2.80**	Any **2** for **$1.86**

[A] **Wavy brush design.** Rayon foulard. *State color.*
33 K 3819G—Blue, maroon, brown, or green$1.47
[B] **"Palm tree."** Rayon-nylon crepe. *State color.*
33 K 3817G—Gray, blue, maroon, or brown $1.47
[C] **"Jumping fish."** Rayon-nylon crepe. *State color.*
33 K 3816G—Red, brown, or blue $1.47
[D] **"Stag."** Rayon and nylon crepe. *State color.*
33 K 3818G—Blue, maroon, or brown . . .$1.47
[E] **"Flying ducks."** Rayon crepe. *State color.*
33 K 3815G—Brown, maroon, or blue 97c
[F] **Initial tie.** Rayon crepe. All initials, except I, O, Q, U, V, X, Y, Z. Also in crest design (no initial)—suitable for anyone. *State color. Print initial or state crest.*
33 K 3814G—Green, blue, or maroon 97c
[G] **"Horse's head."** Rayon crepe. *State color.*
33 K 3813G—Maroon, blue, brown, or green .97c

[A]	[B]	[C]	[D]	[E]
$1.47	$1.47	$1.47	$1.47	97c

[F]	[G]
97c	97c

[B], [C], and [D] Hand-painted in California

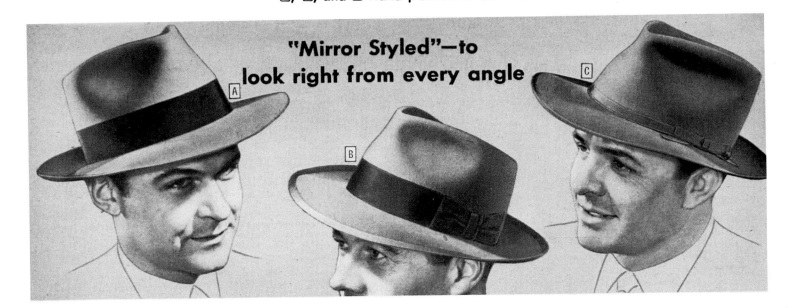

"Mirror Styled"—to
look right from every angle

[A] [B] [C]

Kerrybrooke
THE RIGHT WAY
TO SAY
FASHIONS

[B] $18.98

[C] $16.98

[D] $17.98

[A] $17.98

NEW, DIFFERENT
Big Checks, Bold Plaids
in springweight tweed toppers . . all with the stamp of
fashion approval in their clean-cut, carefree, colorful lines

EVERY COAT RAYON LINED

Two styles of Toppers in checks

The homey, intimate, friendly appeal of nice, big checked tweed . . you'll love it for its long, rugged wear, its lasting good looks, its adaptability to your every mood . . at home in either town or country, over silks or denims. Here we offer this lovely, versatile checked tweed (50% wool and 50% rayon) in two smart toppers . . both fully rayon twill lined, both in *Misses' sizes* 10, 12, 14, 16, 18, 20. Size chart, page 117. *State size.* Shpg. wt. each 3 lbs. 4 oz.

[A] Casual style with long roll collar, blunt lapels, slash pockets, flared back. (about 30 inches long.)
017 K 3622—Navy and pink check.... $17.98
017 K 3623—Navy and gold check..... 17.98
017 K 3624—Brown and gold check.... 17.98

[B] The Double Breasted tie belt casual with stitched, shirred bloused back. (About 32 inches long.)
017 K 3625—Navy and pink check....$18.98
017 K 3626—Navy and gold check..... 18.98
017 K 3627—Brown and gold check.... 18.98

Two styles of Toppers in bold plaid

Plaid . . big and bold . . with all the spice, vitality and color interest of those gay horse blankets of yesteryear . . a current fashion success on city street, on country road, on college campus . . wherever you see smart toppers with a distinctly sports flavor. You'll welcome this fresh approach to a well-balanced wardrobe that gives you an interesting fabric and pattern change from your usual solids and monotones. Both of the 50% wool and 50% rayon toppers listed below are fully rayon twill lined and have convertible cuffs and both are in *Misses' sizes* 10, 12, 14, 16, 18. Size chart, page 117. *Please state size.* Shpg. wt. each 3 lbs. 2 oz.

[C] Double breasted flared back style. Wear open or buttoned. (About 26 inches long.)
017 K 3628—Navy, white, gold plaid
017 K 3629—Brown, white, gold plaid
Each............................$16.98

[D] Extremely simple collarless style with flared back. (About 32 inches long.)
017 K 3630—Navy, white, gold plaid
017 K 3631—Brown, white, gold plaid
Each............................$17.98

Check skirt
and jacket

Red vest and
navy skirt

Check vest
and skirt

Check jacket
with red skirt
and red vest

Check jacket
and skirt with
red vest

It's a SUIT . . It's an ENSEMBLE . .
It's SEPARATES . . for EVERY SEASON

√ **FULLY RAYON LINED CHECK JACKET**

√ **MATCHING CHECK SKIRT**

√ **REVERSIBLE VEST**

√ **SOLID NAVY SKIRT**

√ **SOLID RED SKIRT**

all 5 pieces for only **$26.50** Cash
$3 down, $5 monthly

Our marvelous 5-piece Suit in crease-resistant
year 'round rayon check and fine rayon gabardine

Our wonderful, versatile 5-piece wardrobe suit has so much to recommend it, that we barely
cover the highlights here. First, it's a dead ringer for a famous fashion suit at twice the price;
second, you can wear it any season . . light enough for summer as a two-piecer, ideal for spring
and fall as a three-piecer, and it fits smoothly under your coats for winter. Mix, match or mate
it to your heart's content; over 20 different ways to use the various pieces, but its combinations
are limitless if you team individual pieces with other items in your wardrobe. It's the smartest,
shrewdest investment in apparel you could possibly make. Jacket has hand-set shoulder
pads and beautiful rayon twill lining. Suave-sleek skirts boast neat slits. Vest is check on
one side, red gabardine on the other, with removable stud buttons. Jacket length about 25 in.
Misses' sizes 10, 12, 14, 16, 18, 20. Size chart on page 117. *State size.* Shpg. wt. 4 lbs. 6 oz.
017 K 5421—Jacket and skirt in navy blue and white check with red overplaid: check and
bright red vest; bright red skirt and navy blue skirt . . . . 5 pieces $26.50

Kerrybrooke
THE RIGHT WAY
TO SAY
FASHIONS

$1.98   **$2.29**   **$1.98**

Washable Sunsuits .. Sanforized .. won't shrink over 1%

HIGH-COUNT COTTON BROAD-CLOTH sunsuit has pink midriff with fluffy ruffles of pink and blue edged with white embroidery lace, button back. Blue front-pleated shorts button at side. Washfast. *Girls' sizes 7, 8, 10, 12, 14. State size.* Shpg. wt. 8 oz. 077 K 5510—Pink and blue. $1.98

SANFORIZED SEERSUCKER, elastic neckline and midriff bottom. Shorts with two pockets. Navy piping. Washable .. needs no ironing. *Girls' sizes 7, 8, 10, 12, 14. Please state size.* Shipping weight 9 ounces. 077 K 5511—Red, white..$2.29 077 K 5512—Blue, white. 2.29

HARDY DENIM SUNSUIT has elastic neck, bottom on ruffled midriff. Shorts with elastic-shirred waist, pocket. White cotton pique trim. Washable. *State size 7, 8, 10, 12, 14.* Shpg. wt. 10 oz. 077 K 5513—Shrimp pink 077 K 5514—Med. blue Each...............$1.98

SANFORIZED DENIM
4-Piece Outfit

At a Sears low price
You get all this . . .

- Sanforized plaid gingham shirt to tuck in or out
- Plaid gingham roller hat to wear with everything
- Sanforized denim shorts trimmed with gingham
- Sanforized denim midriff top with gingham ruffle
- The outfit guaranteed not to shrink over 1%

ALL 4 FOR ONLY $4⁹⁸

Your summer-fun wardrobe gives you all this . . . (1) *In-or-outer shirt* of woven gingham plaid with slit tails that can tie in front, too. (2) *Perky roller hat* to match is well-made with stitched brim. (3) *Boxer-style denim shorts* with gay woven gingham plaid cuffs, hip pocket. Snug, stay-put elastic waistband. (4) *Denim midriff* with elastic neckline and bottom .. can be worn on or off shoulder. Frilly ruffle of plaid woven gingham. All Sanforized, washable (maximum fabric shrinkage 1%). *Sizes 7, 8, 10, 12, 14. Please state size.* Shpg. wt. 1 lb. 4 oz. 077 K 5200—Medium blue denim with multicolor plaid.....$4.98

COTTON 3-PIECER

Washfast harlequin check with white cotton pique

all 3 pieces for only $3⁹⁸

YOU GET ALL THIS:

1. Strapless sundress
2. Cute bolero midriff
3. Action-cut shorts

Priced very low at Sears for this quality fashion.

Crisp white cotton pique combined with a dazzling 80-square cotton harlequin check. Halter sundress has figurewise, elasticized bodice, a wide-swirling skirt. Bolero midriff ties in bow, is trimmed with checks. Shorts are front-pleated, have smartly checked cuffs. All washfast. *Girls' sizes 7, 8, 10, 12, 14. Please state size.* Shipping weight 1 pound 3 oz. 077 K 5201—White pique with red and white checks Outfit...........$3.98

$1.98 (A)
$2.98 (B)
$2.49 (C)
$2.29 (D)
$1.98 (E)

WASHABLE COTTON SUN DRESSES.. SIZES 7 TO 14.. especially designed

for school-age girls . . bolero ensembles to wear now and all summer

[A] WASHFAST 80-SQ. PERCALE dress with separate bolero. Elastic shirring at bodice top and waist. Bolero and skirt ruffle match background of print. A wonderful value at only $1.98. *Sizes 7, 8, 10, 12, 14. State size. Shpg. wt. 9 oz.*
077K2036–Red with gray and white
077K2037–Medium blue with navy and white print . . . . Each $1.98

[C] WASHFAST BROADCLOTH dress with matching bolero. Adorable dress with white piping, button straps, tie-back sash. Separate bolero with piping and ruffle sleeves. *Sizes 7, 8, 10, 12, 14. Shpg. wt. 9 oz.*
077 K 2038–Blue border, multicolor print. *State size* . . . . Each $2.49
077 K 2039–Rose border, multicolor print. *State size* . . . . Each $2.49

[E] WASHFAST 80-SQ. PERCALE . . multicolor print. Elastic shirring at waist and top . . ruffle can be worn off shoulders. Swing skirt (about 110 in.). *Sizes 7, 8, 10, 12, 14. Measure; state size. Shpg. wt. 8 oz.*
077 K 2031–Rose ground $1.98
077 K 2032–Med. blue ground 1.98

Striped and polka dot sun dresses $1.49 each, 2 for $2.78
BOTH IN WASHFAST 80-SQ. PERCALE. One-piece striped dress has elastic shirring at bodice top and around waist. Two-piece polka dot dress has elastic shirring at top of skirt and at top and bottom of midriff (wear on or off shoulders). The midriff looks well with dungarees; the skirt with blouses. Save by buying one for $1.49; save more by buying two (2 of 1 style or 1 of each). *Sizes 7, 8, 10, 12, 14. Shpg. wt. ea. 8 oz.*

[G] One-piece striped sun dress
077 K 2027–Bright red and white
077 K 2028–Medium blue and white
State size. Each $1.49; 2 for $2.78

[H] Two-piece polka dot sun dress
077 K 2029–Bright red and white
077 K 2030–Medium blue and white
State size. Each $1.49; 2 for $2.78

[B] SANFORIZED, WASHFAST BROADCLOTH dress with matching bolero. Contrast color front yoke with lovely white embroidery. Piping on bolero matches yoke. *Sizes 7, 8, 10, 12, 14. Shpg. wt. 9 oz.*
077 K 2041–Light blue with royal
077K2042–Medium pink with brown
Measure; state size . . . . . Each $2.98

[D] SANFORIZED, WASHABLE BROADCLOTH with ruffles and inserts of pretty white eyelet embroidery. Button back. *Sizes 7, 8, 10, 12, 14. Measure; state size. Shpg. wt. 8 oz.*
077 K 2033–Medium Blue . . $2.29
077 K 2034–Pink 2.29
077 K 2035–Yellow 2.29

[F] WASHFAST EMBOSSED COTTON . . crisp, expensive looking with a raised criss-cross design; won't shrink more than 2%, needs little or no ironing. A beautiful outfit. Dress has white bodice with cuffed front, swing skirt. Bolero has white collar and cuffs. *Sizes 7, 8, 10, 12, 14. State size. Shpg. wt. 1 lb. 2 oz.*
077 K 2044–Aqua blue $4.19
077 K 2045–Yellow 4.19

[F] $4.19

$1.49 EACH 2 FOR $2.78

[G]   [H]

Our Finest Kerrybrookes IN JUNIORS' SIZES

For the young figure with small, high bustline and slim, well defined waistline. Our Finest Kerrybrookes fit better and look smarter because they're made better.

B
$15.98
Also
Misses' Sizes
10 to 20

C
**DRESS
and JACKET
ENSEMBLE**
$10.98
Also
Misses' Sizes
10 to 16

[C] OUR FINEST RAYON FAILLE .. new sheath dress for early and late evening parties; jacket to make a wonderful daytime ensemble. Scallops all around top of dress .. on collar, down front and all around perky peplum of jacket. Dress has narrow shoulder straps (not shown), 4-gore skirt with 2-inch hem, ⅞-inch side-seams. Dry clean. *Juniors' sizes 9, 11, 13, 15, 17; Misses' sizes 10, 12, 14, 16 only. Measure; order correct size.* Shpg. wt. 1 lb. 10 oz.
031 D 9010–Aqua blue   031 D 9011–Pink rose
031 D 9012–Black . . . . Each $10.98

FORMAL GOWNS for weddings and the most important parties of the season .. juniors' and misses' sizes

← [A] FINE QUALITY IMPORTED RAYON NET .. bodice of beautiful Alencon-type rayon lace, dyed to match, studded with sparkling rhinestones. The big American beauty rose and the separate net stole are included to make a complete outfit that's truly glamorous. The bodice has a front overdrape of net .. can be worn with its taffeta shoulder straps or without (lightweight boning holds it securely). The skirt is double (2 layers of net) with matching horsehair around the bottom to make it stand out. Bodice lining and attached underskirt are matching rayon taffeta. Dry clean. *Juniors' sizes 9, 11, 13, 15, 17; Misses' sizes 10, 12, 14, 16, 18. Order correct size.* Shpg. wt. 1 lb. 1 oz.
031 D 9000–White   031 D 9001–Pink
031 D 9002–Aqua blue . . . . Each $15.98

[B] SLIPPER SATIN .. a lustrous, heavy rayon with bodice and slip-on gloves of exquisite Alencon-type rayon lace, dyed to match. This is a one-piece evening dress that is easy to wear, requires no special accessories or undergarments. It is very flattering to every age and figure .. looks far more than its reasonable price. The satin skirt is very full, gathered all around. The bodice and the flared, all-around peplum are lined with matching satin. Button ornaments are satin covered with lace. Dry clean. *Juniors' sizes 9, 11, 13, 15, 17; also Misses' sizes 10, 12, 14, 16, 18, 20. Please see size charts on the preceding page. Measure; order your correct size.* Shpg. wt. 1 lb. 13 oz.
031 D 9005–Light gold   031 D 9006–White
031 D 9007–Nile (light) green . . . . Each $15.98

[A] **$15.98**
Also Misses' Sizes 10 to 18

A $6.98 Sizes 12 to 20

B $9.69 Sizes 10 to 18

C $9.49 Sizes 12 to 20

D $9.49 Sizes 12 to 20

E $7.59 Sizes 12 to 20

OUR BEST TAFFETA .. rustling, crisp rayon .. smooth textured, dressy

FINE RIBBED CREPE .. soft draping, heavy rayon sheer for year 'round wear

A Surplice neckline, skirt with front overdrape and big bow .. wonderful for your figure. Collar can be worn up or down; back half-belt keeps waistline snug. 7/8-inch seams for easy alteration; 2-inch hem. Rayon taffeta; dry clean. *Misses' sizes* 12, 14, 16, 18, 20. *Measure; order correct size.* Shipping wt. 14 oz.
031 D 9492—Black
031 D 9493—Deep gold
031 D 9494—Deep violet
Each $6.98

B Beautiful collar and cuffs of white fur-like fabric, full circle skirt .. a dress that's dramatic, yet easy to wear. You can remove the collar and cuffs and wear it with jewelry .. it looks like an entirely different dress. Narrow taped hem. Rayon taffeta; dry clean. *Misses' sizes* 10, 12, 14, 16, 18. *Order correct size.* Shpg. wt. 1 lb. 3 oz.
031 D 9477—Black
031 D 9478—Navy blue
Each $9.69

C Front draped neckline .. full skirt with pointed yoke in front and back. This dress is young looking, becoming to every type of figure. Back zipper, 7/8-inch sideseams for easy alteration, 1-inch taped hem. Fine ribbed rayon crepe; dry clean. *Misses' sizes* 12, 14, 16, 18, 20. *Order correct size.* Shpg. wt. 1 lb. 4 oz.
031 D 9471—Black
031 D 9472—Ruby (deep) red
031 D 9473—Teal (medium) blue . . . . Each $9.49

D Openwork neckline of corded fabric .. bands that go all around the skirt, dip to a V in back. Wonderful for the slim or medium figure. Narrow 1-piece skirt, shirred below back waist. Back zipper .. 2-inch taped hem. Ribbed rayon crepe; dry clean. *Misses' sizes* 12, 14, 16, 18, 20. *Please measure; order correct size.* Shpg. wt. 1 lb. 1 oz.
031D9474—Black $9.49
031D9475—Navy blue . . 9.49
031D9476—Dark green . . 9.49

OUR MOST BEAUTIFUL CREPE .. fine quality rayon

E This dress looks wonderful on everybody. Tucks give flattering bustline fullness .. skirt has pockets, front pleats, 3-gore back. 7/8-inch sideseams for easy alteration, 2-inch hem. Beautiful, finely ribbed rayon that looks like silk; dry clean. *Misses' sizes* 12, 14, 16, 18, 20. Shpg. wt. 1 lb. 1 oz.
031 D 9468—Black
031 D 9470—Taupe (medium) brown
031 D 9469—Teal (medium) blue
Order correct size. . . . . . Each $7.59

Kerrybrooke

THE **RIGHT** WAY
TO SAY

FASHIONS

$27.98 cash
$3 down, $5 monthly

$27.98 cash
$3 down, $5 monthly

$29.98 cash
$3 down, $5 monthly

TO WRAP YOU in stylish luxury . . our newest wrap-around creation with figure-enhancing back interest that begins with the new button-trimmed contour belt and continues with a cascade of rippling fullness to the hemline. New wide, stand-up collar is convertible. Rayon satin lined, warmly interlined. Another outstanding buy in our ripple weave all wool suede cloth. *Misses' sizes* 10, 12, 14, 16, 18, 20.

017 D 3775—Bright red   017 D 3777—Gold
017 D 3776—Rum (rust brown)   017 D 3778—Navy blue
Shipping weight 5 pounds 6 ounces . . . . . Each **$27.98**

MODIFIED PYRAMID. Easy-fitting, conservative interpretation of the new pyramid . . giving you the glamorous sweeping pyramid flared effect without that noticeable fullness. Wonderful value in our wonder-wearing ripple weave suede cloth. Lined with matching rayon satin, warmly interlined.
Misses' sizes 10, 12, 14, 16, 18, 20. Be sure to measure for proper fit.

017 D 3780—Bright red   017 D 3782—Gold
017 D 3781—Rum (rust brown)   017 D 3783—Navy blue
Shipping weight 5 pounds . . . . Each **$27.98**

SENSATIONAL STYLE SUCCESS . . the arrowhead and velvet trimmed full pyramid, this year's most wanted coat fashion. Full, sweeping, billowy . . yards and yards of our ripple-weave all wool suede envelop you in stylish luxury for a tiny price. Underside of stand-up collar and arrowpoints are rayon velvet. Nicely lined with matching rayon satin; interlined. *Misses' sizes* 10, 12, 14, 16, 18, 20.

017 D 3785—Bright red   017 D 3787—Gold
017 D 3786—Rum (rust brown)   017 D 3788—Navy blue
Shipping weight 5 pounds . . . . Each **$29.98**

F $8.90
Black or
brown suede,
calfskin trim

G $7.98
Black or
turf tan
calfskin

HIGH HEEL

MEDIUM HEEL

Tailored Elegance

Mellow, longer life calfskin, polished to a fine warm luster; whisper-soft, exciting suede

[F] You'll look far to find better walking shoes, such good companions for fall suits. Lush suede; bright calfskin at toe, across instep. Wheeled extension edge leather sole, 2¼-inch heels.
Sizes: AA (narrow) width in 5½, 6, 6½, 7, 7½, 8, 8½, 9 and 10.
Sizes: B (medium) width in 4½, 5, 5½, 6, 6½, 7, 7½, 8, 8½, 9. *Please state size and width.* Shipping weight 1 lb. 9 oz.
54 D 8622—Black suede, calf ....Pair $8.90
54 D 8623—Brown suede, calf ...Pair 8.90

[H] Dressmaker touch, scalloped throat line. Deep cut at sides. Leather sole.
Sizes: AA (narrow) width in 6, 6½, 7, 7½, 8, 8½, 9 and 10.
Sizes: B (medium) width in 5, 5½, 6, 6½, 7, 7½, 8, 8½, 9 and 10. *Please state size and width.* Shipping wt. 1 lb. 9 oz.
2¾-inch high heels
54 D 8732—Black suede ....Pair $7.98
54 D 8733—Black calfskin ......Pair 7.98
54 D 8734—Brown calfskin .....Pair 7.98
1¾-inch medium heels
54 D 8735—Black suede ....Pair $7.98
54 D 8736—Black calfskin ......Pair 7.98
54 D 8737—Brown calfskin .....Pair 7.98

[K] The crisp lines you love in spectators. They fit with easy grace, walk tirelessly through busy days, go with everything. Calfskin, perforated and pinked wall toe and back. Stitched extension edge leather sole, 2-inch heel.
Sizes: AA (narrow) width in 5½, 6, 6½, 7, 7½, 8, 8½, 9, 9½ and 10.
Sizes: B (medium) in 4½, 5, 5½, 6, 6½, 7, 7½, 8, 8½, 9, 9½ and 10. *Please state size and width.* Shipping. wt. 1 lb. 9 oz.
54 D 8552—Black calfskin ......Pair $7.98
54 D 8553—Saddle brown calf...Pair 7.98

[G] Slenderizing envelope vamp swings high over instep; a small buckled vamp strap. Open toe, bare back, adjustable sling strap. Stitched extension edge leather sole, 2⅛-inch heel.
Sizes: B (medium) width in 4½, 5, 5½, 6, 6½, 7, 7½, 8, 8½ and 9.
Sizes: C (medium wide) width in 5, 5½, 6, 6½, 7, 7½, 8, 8½ and 9. *Please state size and width.* Shpg. wt. 1 lb. 9 oz.
54 D 8782—Black calfskin ......Pair $7.98
54 D 8783—Turf tan calfskin.....Pair 7.98

[J] Lustrous calfskin pump, as much at home with mink as with tweeds; you'll make it the mainstay of your shoe wardrobe from sun-up to sun-down. Squared at toe and heel, wall-lasted for more toe room. Rope stitched oval vamp ornament at the throat. Stitched extension edge leather sole. 2⅛-inch heel.
Sizes: AA (narrow) width in 6 to 10.
Sizes: B (medium) width in 4½ to 9. Half sizes too. *Please state size and width.* Shipping weight 1 pound 9 ounces.
54 D 8674—Black calfskin ......Pair $7.98
54 D 8675—Brown calfskin ......Pair 7.98

[L] Our finest Kerrybrooke quality. High in front slip-on; a slim padded strap crosses the U-throat. Rope-stitched, ridged vamp, easy-feeling last. Polished calfskin in warm reddish brown or black. Extension edge leather sole, underscored with white stitching, 2-inch heel. Foot-flattering charmer with a talent for traveling here, there and everywhere.
Sizes: B (med.) 4½, 5, 5½, 6 6½, 7, 7½, 8, 8½, 9. *State size.* Shpg. wt. 1 lb. 9 oz.
54 D 8680—Black calfskin ......Pair $8.90
54 D 8681—Reddish brown calf .Pair 8.90

H $7.98
Black suede:
black or
brown calfskin

J $7.98
Black or
brown calfskin

K $7.98
Black or
saddle
brown calfskin

L $8.90
Black or
brown calfskin

SANFORIZED
COTTON

SANFORIZED
COTTON

Nautical SAILCLOTH

4-Pc. Kerrybrooke Boxed Wardrobe
Skipper blue and white nautical style
Skirt, Weskit, Shorts and Visor Cap

$10.98
Complete

Firm, spick and span, fun to wear. The blue is bright, the white dazzling, with neat navy blue braid and rope belt. **Sleeveless White Weskit** buttons snug. **Four Gore Skirt** zips in back, has two stunning pockets, rope belt. **Shorts** are cuffed, with pockets like the skirt, rope belt. Back zipper. **Visor Cap** is blue sailcloth. Washable, max. fab. shrink. 1%. *State Misses' sizes* 10, 12, 14, 16, 18. Shpg. wt. 2 lbs. 5 oz.
07 K 628—Skipper blue and white 4-pc. outfit, boxed. **$10.98**

Leaf Print WITH TANGERINE

4-Piece Kerrybrooke Boxed Wardrobe makes 4 outfits
Flared Print Skirt, Sun Bra, Tangerine Blouse, Shorts
All you need for a smart weekend . . made for Sears alone

$8.98
Complete

It's a striking palm leaf print in shades of gold, blue and tangerine. With it we put solid tangerine, beautiful for blondes, brunettes or redheads, handsome with suntan. It's a 4-piece wardrobe to fill a weekend with compliments. **Print Skirt** flares wide with front gathers, zipper in back. Concealed side pocket. **Blouse** is tangerine broadcloth with mandarin collar. Ties at waist. **Shorts** are tangerine with cuffs, back zipper. **Sun Bra** is print lined with tangerine. Center drawstring forms shoulder straps. Buttons in back. Washable, max. fab. shrink. 1%. *Misses' sizes* 10, 12, 14, 16, 18. *Please state size.* Shipping weight 1 lb. 10 oz.
07 K 629—Print and tangerine 4-piece wardrobe . . . . Each outfit **$8.98**

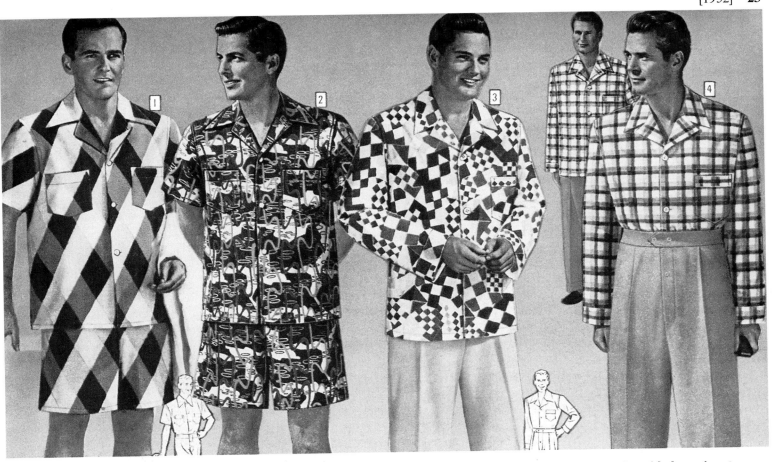

NEW "SPORT SHORTY" . . it's both Pajama and Sport Suit **PILGRIM SLACK PAJAMAS . . for comfortable lounging, too**

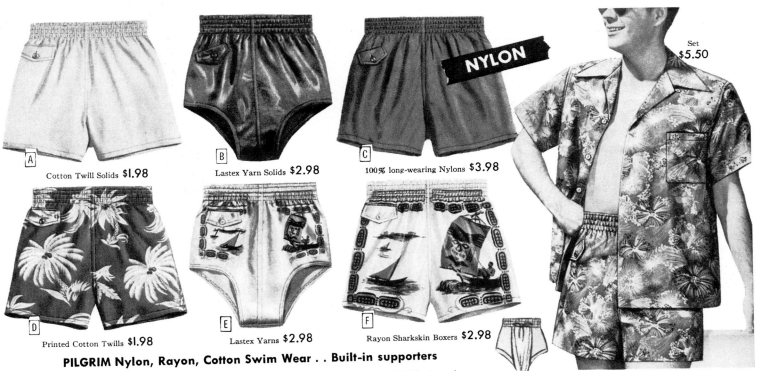

Set $5.50

NYLON

Cotton Twill Solids **$1.98**   Lastex Yarn Solids **$2.98**   100% long-wearing Nylons **$3.98**

Printed Cotton Twills **$1.98**   Lastex Yarns **$2.98**   Rayon Sharkskin Boxers **$2.98**

PILGRIM Nylon, Rayon, Cotton Swim Wear . . Built-in supporters

A, C, D, F: *Sizes* small (28-30-in. waist); medium (32-34); med. large (36-38); large (40-42). *State size.*

[A] **Cotton Twill.** Vat-dyed colors. Sanforized . . . won't shrink over 1%. Knit acetate supporter. Flap pocket.
33 H 2330—Tan   Shpg. wt. 8 oz.
33 H 2331—Maroon *State size.*
33 H 2332—Royal blue   Each **$1.98**

[D] **Bright All-over Printed Cotton Twill.** Same features above. Full acetate supporter. Elastic waistband, drawstring. Shpg. wt. 8 oz. *State size.*
33H2333—Maroon; blue, white
33H2334—Gray; maize, white.   **$1.98**

[B] **Rayon Lastex yarn solids.** Rayon supporter. *Sizes* small (28-30-in.); med. (32-34); med. large (36-38).
33 H 2345—Royal blue   Wt. 8 oz.
33 H 2346—Maroon *State size.*
33 H 2347—Gold color. Each **$2.98**

[E] **Printed Tribal Design. Acetate Lastex yarn.** Fine details. *Sizes* small (28-30-in. waist); med. (32-34); med. large (36-38). Wt. 8 oz.
33H2335—White ground
33H2336—Maize ground Each **$2.98**

[C] **100% Nylon;** long-wearing. Elastic waist, drawstring. Full supporter 100% nylon.
33H2309—Green. *State size.*
33H2310—Royal blue. Shpg. wt. 7 oz.
33H2311—Maroon
33H2312—Gray . . . . . Each **$3.98**

[F] **Boxer style Tribal Print** on rayon sharkskin. Rayon supporter. *State size.* Shpg. wt. 8 oz.
33 H 2337—Tan
33 H 2338—Maize . . Each **$2.98**

Sturdy Panel supporters on B, E.

Full supporters
A, D, C, F.

NEW PILGRIM BEACH SET

Exciting, vat-dyed multicolored pattern printed on lustrous acetate crepe. **Trunks.** All lined plus full rayon supporter. *Sizes* small (28-30-in. waist); med. (32-34); med. large (36-38); large (40-42). Wt. 7 oz. *State size.*
33 H 2339—Green ground
33 H 2340—Gray ground Each **$2.98**

Matching Sport Shirt. Button front, pocket. *Sizes* small (14-14½-in. neck); med. (15-15½); med. large (16-16½); large (17-17½). Wt. 7 oz. *State size.*
33 H 2341—Green ground
33 H 2342—Gray ground Each **$2.98**

Save 46c. Order by the Set. Shpg. wt. 14 oz. *State sizes above.*
33 H 2343—Green ground
33 H 2344—Gray ground Set **$5.50**

Sanforized DENIM DUNGAREES

Sears Famous WESTERN-STYLE

Teens' Sizes 10 to 16

Girls' Sizes 7 to 14

BIG VALUES at Sears Low Prices

Made to Sears own rigid specifications

Side-zip style features:

- Max. fab. shrinkage 1%
- Two front inside swing pockets with copper-riveted corners to prevent ripping
- Gripper fastener waist
- Back yoke for trim lines
- Two back pockets firmly bar-tacked at corners
- Zipper placket at side
- Double-needle orange stitching throughout
- 5 bar-tacked belt loops
- All inside seams neatly finished . . . no raw edges

Boxer-style features:

- Max. fab. shrinkage 1%
- Elastic-shirred waistband
- Copper rivets reinforce 2 deep front pockets
- Bar-tacked back pocket
- Sleek yoke in the back
- Double-needle orange stitching throughout
- All inside seams neatly finished . . . no raw edges

GIRLS' BOXER-STYLE JEANS

$1.54 6-oz. denim only

[A] Another famous blue denim classic with all the Sears features girls love (see above). Snug elastic shirred waistline stays put. Wash separately.
State Girls' sizes 7, 8, 10, 12, 14. Size chart, page 109.
77 H 5303—Navy blue. Shpg. wt. 11 oz. **$1.54**

[D] Top-Button Sanforized Denim Crew Cap 98c
The perfect team mate with her jeans . . cute-as-a-button crew cap. Navy blue with orange stitching.
078 H 4100—Fits 20¾-21¼ in. Shpg. wt. 5 oz. . . . **98c**
078 H 4101—Fits 21½-22¼ in. Shpg. wt. 5 oz. . . . **98c**

SIDE-ZIP DENIMS FOR GIRLS

$1.79 6-oz. denim   **$1.98** 8-oz. denim

[B] Sears denims are girls' favorites for knock-about wear from coast-to-coast . . . and for good reason . . . our famous features make them more rugged, better-looking (see specifications above). Wash separately. *Girls' sizes 7, 8, 10, 12, 14. State size. Size chart, page 109.*
Firm 6-ounce denim. Shipping weight 13 oz.
77 H 5326—Navy blue. **$1.79**
Durable 8-ounce Denim. Shipping weight 15 oz.
77 H 5343—Navy blue. **$1.98**

SIDE-ZIP DENIMS FOR TEENS

$1.89 6-oz. denim   **$2.29** 8-oz. denim

[C] Sears blue denims are done to a Teen's taste . . sleek-waisted, with hug-the-hips lines, action-styling throughout. All the details of famous classics make them better-wearing, better-looking (see features above). Wash separately.
State Teens' sizes 10, 12, 14, 16. Size chart, page 118.
Firm 6-ounce denim. Shpg. wt. 1 lb. 2 oz.
77 H 6326—Navy blue. **$1.89**
Rugged 8-ounce denim. Shpg. wt. 1 lb. 4 oz.
77 H 6343—Navy blue. **$2.29**

GUARANTEED TO FIT

.. Copper-Rivet Reinforced

"Jewel" Decorated Jet Black Denim

[A] Frontier style Sanforized black denim jeans (1% max. shrinkage). Narrow-cut legs with large cuff turn-up. Zipper fly front. 2 boatsail drill front pockets with cluster of nickel plated studs and imitation jewels. 2 hip pockets with western design white embroidered loop. Wash alone. No belt. *State Size* 4, 6, 8, 10, 12. See size chart below.
50 H 9165M—Jeans. Shpg. wt. 1 lb. 3 oz.... $2.19

Jeans or Jacket $2.19 Ea.

MATCHING JACKET of 8-oz. Sanforized black denim; (1% max. shrinkage). Pleated front, back. 2 pockets. Snap-fastener front, cuffs. Wash alone. *State size* 4, 6, 8, 10, 12. See chart on page 1289.
50 H 9166M—Jacket. Shpg. wt. 1 lb. 3 oz.... $2.19

Circle "S" Ranch Blue Denim

[B] Rancher style 7¼-oz. Sanforized blue denim jeans (max. shrinkage 1%). Western decorated with imitation jewels and red trim set against a background of deep blue. Nailhead studs on front. Zipper fly, 4 large pockets. Wash alone. No belt. *State size* 4, 6, 8, 10, 12. See size chart below.
50 H 9124M—Jeans. Shpg. wt. 1 lb. 1 oz.... $1.89

Jeans or Jacket $1.89 Ea.

CIRCLE "S" RANCH JACKET. Matches jeans above. Same Sanforized 7¼-oz. denim (1% max. shrinkage). 2 studded pockets. Snap-fastener front. Bright chest and collar decorations. Wash separately. *State size* 4, 6, 8, 10, 12. See chart page 1289.
50 H 9125M—Jacket. Shpg. wt. 1 lb. 1 oz.... $1.89

Yoke back. Western design on pockets

SPORT SHIRTS .. Full-cut, Colorful, WASHFAST

[B] Washfast Hawaiian Print Sanforized, Mercerized **$1.94**

[C] Plaid and Plain Western of Sanforized Broadcloth **$1.94**

[D] Washfast Colorful Plaid Loop-fastening Collar **$1.59**

WARM COTTON FLANNELS .. Sanforized, WASHFAST

[F] EXTRA HEAVY flannel with Woven-in-Plaid **$1.89**

[G] Popular piped Western Plaid 'n' Plain Flannel **$2.27**

[H] Heavier weight Flannel Plaid, Double Yoke **$1.54**

AUTHENTIC Western-styled *Roy Rogers* Jeans 'n' Jacket

Extra-Tough Sanforized 8-oz. Blue Denim

JEANS $1.95
JACKET $1.95

Heavy-duty Zipper fly — *Western type Yoke Back*

Authentic Roy Rogers Western denims! Approved by Roy .. styled for you ... Sold only at Sears. Rip-resistant tailored of strong 8-oz. Sanforized blue denim (max. shrinkage 1%). Cowboy-style jeans with heavy-duty zip fly; 2 front copper-riveted drill pockets, 2 back patch pockets have embroidered loop design. Roy's own emblem on front; imitation leather patch in back "branded" by Roy. Thread bartacked. Wash alone. No belt. *Sizes* 4, 6, 8, 10, 12. Chart left.
50H9136M—Jeans. Wt. 1 lb. 1 oz. $1.95

MATCHING JACKET of same 8-oz. Sanforized denim as jeans above. Pleated front with snap-fastener closure; Western-action back. Roy's own emblem and imitation leather patch in front. Wash alone. *Sizes* 4, 6, 8, 10, 12. Chart pg. 1289.
50H9137M—Jacket. Wt. 1 lb. 1 oz. $1.95

Kerrybrooke
THE RIGHT WAY
TO SAY
FASHIONS

100% Nylon

A
$9.98
Sizes 9 to 17;
also 10 to 18

B
$10.79
Sizes 9 to 17;
also 10 to 18

100% Nylon

C
$11.98
Sizes 9 to 17

D
$8.98
Sizes 9 to 15
only

OUR FINEST KERRYBROOKES

A Our Best Rayon Taffeta . . glamorous coat dress with separate taffeta petticoat and wonderful new "bell" skirt. Dirndl petticoat is red plaid with crinoline around bottom to make it stand out. Dry clean. *Juniors' sizes 9, 11, 13, 15, 17; Misses' sizes 10, 12, 14, 16, 18. Order correct size.* Shpg. wt. 1 lb. 9 oz.
031H8020–Navy blue $9.98   031H8021–Black $9.98

B 100% Nylon . . smooth, filmy sheer . . needs little or no ironing. Pointed bodice set on to yoke for flattering bustline . . dirndl skirt, 2-inch hem. Fabric loops and buttons. Hand wash separately. *Juniors' sizes 9, 11, 13, 15, 17; also Misses' sizes 10, 12, 14, 16, 18. Order correct size.* Shpg. wt. 14 oz.
031H8015–Navy blue plaid on white ground. . .$10.79
031H8016–Cherry red plaid on white ground. . 10.79
031H8017–Bright green plaid on white ground. 10.79

C 100% Nylon . . an exquisite. finely puckered sheer that's smart for every season, needs little or no ironing, keeps its new look. Winged mandarin collar . . winged cuffs . . rhinestone buttons . . full dirndl skirt with 2-inch hem. 100% Nylon! Hand wash separately. *Juniors' sizes 9, 11, 13, 15, 17. Order correct size.*
031H9029–Turquoise blue   031H9030–Rosebud pink
031H9033–Navy blue. . .Each. Shpg. wt. 1 lb. $11.98

D Rayon Ninon . . very fine, durable net with applied white design that looks like embroidery. Dirndl skirt with pleated ruffle all around; attached slip of matching taffeta. Black velvet sash. Dry clean. *Juniors' sizes 9, 11, 13, 15 only.* Shpg. wt. 1 lb. 6 oz.
031 H 8010 – Petal pink   031 H 8011 – Yellow
031H8012–Aqua blue. *Order correct size.*. . . .Each $8.98

E Our Finest Linen-Like Rayon . . new . . beautiful . . first time in our catalog! Smart dress and cape ensemble. Dress has set-in pockets, 3-gore skirt back, 2-inch hem. Bodice of dress and cape lining are fine printed rayon crepe. Dry clean. *Juniors' sizes 9, 11, 13, 15, 17; Misses' sizes 10, 12, 14, 16, 18. Measure; order correct size.* Shpg. wt. 1 lb. 9 oz.
031H8025–Medium beige with brown and white. $10.49
031H8026–Navy blue with navy and white print. 10.49

E
$10.49
Sizes 9 to 17;
also 10 to 18

. . DRESSES

D
$9.98
Sizes 9 to 17;
also 10 to 18

E
$6.49
Sizes 9 to 15
only

F
$8.98
Sizes 9 to 17;
also 10 to 18

G
$6.39
Sizes
9 to 17

H
$10.49
DRESS AND
COAT ENSEMBLE
Sizes 9 to 17;
also 10 to 18

A MAN-TAILORED SUIT. Easy-fitting smooth lines with the important look of a custom-made suit. Front kick-pleat on 4-gore straight skirt. Team with the coat on opposite page in your own choice of color combinations. Jacket length about 26 in. long. *Misses' sizes 12, 14, 16, 18, 20. Size chart, page 129. Please state size.*

Our Finest 100% Worsted Wool Sheen Gabardine. Shpg. wt. 3 lbs. 5 oz.
017 H 3019—Navy blue......$29.98
017 H 3020—Pastel gold....... 29.98
017 H 3021—Emerald green.... 29.98

Sheen Gabardine (60% rayon, 40% worsted). Shipping weight 3 lbs. 5 oz.
017 H 3022—Navy blue......$21.50
017 H 3023—Pastel gold...... 21.50
017 H 3024—Medium green.... 21.50

Rayon Sheen Gabardine . . stain and crease-resistant. Shipping weight 3 lbs.
017 H 3025—Navy blue......$16.98
017 H 3026—Pastel gold....... 16.98
017 H 3027—Medium green.... 16.98

B PETTICOATS ARE BACK in a big, big way and our doll-waist success suit will give you the opportunity of a lifetime to wear yours . . although it's designed with the petticoat in mind . . with a doll-curved waistline padded hips and a skirt that swings wide and free down to a full 100 inches at the hemline, it's equally becoming over your slips. Jacket length about 23 in. *State Misses' sizes 10, 12, 14, 16, 18, 20.*

Our Finest 100% Worsted Wool Sheen Gabardine. Shpg. wt. 3 lbs. 6 oz.
017 H 3028—Navy blue
017 H 3029—Violet
017 H 3030—Spanish (bright) red
017 H 3031—Light gray. Each $29.98

Sheen Gabardine (60% rayon, 40% worsted). Shpg. wt. 3 lbs. 4 oz.
017 H 3032—Navy blue
017 H 3033—Lilac
017 H 3034—Spanish (bright) red
017 H 3035—Light gray. Each $21.50

Rayon Sheen Gabardine . . stain and crease-resistant. Shpg. wt. 3 lbs. 1 oz.
017 H 3036—Navy blue
017 H 3037—Lilac
017 H 3038—Spanish (bright) red
017 H 3039—Light gray. Each $16.98

Sheen Gabardines

1. All worsted wool and blended fabrics won't shrink out of shape; all rayon fabrics are laboratory-tested by Sears for water-repellency, crease-resistance and resistance to non-oil and non-fat stains

2. All sizes scientifically proportioned for proper fit

3. Full canvas in front and collar for smooth appearance

4. All jackets and coats fully lined with fine, matching rayon crepe

5. Shoulder pads hand-set

6. All buttonholes are handmade

7. Skirts have "Snug-Tex" waistbands (a special facing not affected by perspiration, dry cleaning or pressing) to keep your blouse neatly tucked in

8. All skirts have concealed side zippers for quick dressing

9. Generous seams and hems . . if alterations are necessary

10. Seams are pinked and pressed flat so they won't unravel

11. Sears quality controlled . . all garments rigidly inspected

Kerrybrooke

THE RIGHT WAY TO SAY

FASHIONS

FOR A SMART BUY
.. ORDER

Our Best Bags

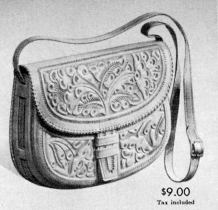

$9.00
Tax included

Hand Made Imported Bag

Every inch of this top grain cowhide bag is made by hand. Yes, hand tooled, hand laced, hand sewn . . even hand dyed. Adjustable shoulderstrap. Unlined. Made in Guatemala. Abt. 9¾x7½ in. Wt.1 lb.3 oz.

88 H 659E—Tan	88 H 660E—Brown
88 H 661E—Black	88 H 672E—Red
88 H 1844E—Navy	Each.....$9.00

$6.00
Tax included

Genuine Corde Scallop-Top Bag

So luxurious, so dressy in genuine corde, enriched with self-embroidery and topped with fashion-smart scalloping. Practical assets . . two deep side pockets, zipper top. Rayon lined. About 10½x5¾ in. Shipping weight 1 lb. 1 oz.

88 H 1823E—Black	88 H 1824E—Brown
88 H 1825E—Navy	Each......$6.00

$1.98

$5.00
Tax included

Western Roll Bag and Belt . . in saddle leather

Casual partners to wear with skirts, suits, dresses. Sparkling gold-color metal horseshoe ornaments . . lucky fashion omens . . on adjustable shoulderstrap bag in saddle leather. Unlined. About 9x5 in. Matching contour belt adjusts to fit sizes 24 to 32.

[A] *Bag.* Gold-colored metal turn lock. Wt. 1 lb. 3 oz.
88 H 1828ME—Black....$5.00
88 H 1829ME—Saddle tan 5.00
88 H 1830ME—Red 5.00
88 H 1831ME—Navy blue 5.00

[B] *Belt.* Front about 2 in. wide. Shpg. wt. 5 oz.
88 H 1832M—Black $1.98
88 H 1833M—Saddle tan . 1.98
88 H 1834M—Red....... 1.98
88 H 1835M—Navy blue.. 1.98

$6.00
Tax included

Carry the Covered Wagon Bag

Sheer fashion genius. A western covered wagon inspired this rich top grain cowhide bag beauty. Inside zipper pocket. Covered metal frame coin purse, mirror. Rayon lined. About 8½x4 in.

88 H 1840E—Black	88 H 1841E—Red
88 H 1842E—Navy	88 H 1843E—Saddle tan
Shpg. wt. 14 oz.............Each $6.00	

$6.50
Tax included

The Kerrybrooke Frame Bag

Made for Sears alone. In rich top grain leather with front zip pocket that forms a wall pocket for your handkerchiefs, gloves, etc. Two deep side pockets, covered metal frame coin purse. Rayon lined. About 9¾x7¼ in. Shpg. wt. 1 lb. 9 oz.
88 H 1018E—Black   88 H 1019E—Brown
88 H 949E—Navy blue......Each $6.50

$5.89
Tax included

The Tambourine Bag in Nylon Faille or Guimpe

Glitters with gold-color metal trim. Rich interior with rayon faille lining. Coin purse. Mirror. About 7x7 in. Wt. 1 lb. 5 oz.
In Nylon Faille. Long-wearing fabric so easy-to-clean.
88 H 1836E—Black..$5.89   88 H 1837E—Navy blue..$5.89
Also in rayon and cotton Guimpe—looks like genuine corde.
88 H 1838E—Black..$5.89   88 H 1839E—Brown.....$5.89

$9.00
Tax included

2-in-1 Reptile Shoulder Bag

Unsnap shoulderstrap converter for a drawstring pouch. Now look at the carefully stitched reptile squares of precious snakeskin and lizagator. Rayon lined. About 9x9 in. Shpg. wt. 1 lb. 4 oz.
88 H 1821E—Navy   88 H 1822E—Brown
88 H 1820E—Multicolored ......Each $9.00

Price of Handbags include 20% Federal Excise Tax.

GLEAMING LETTERS, all but "X". Print letters wanted. Size 1⅛ inches. Shipping weight each 1 ounce.
88 H 1012M—Gold-color metal.......Each 29c; 3 for 84c

$6.50
Tax included

Trim Satchel in Saddle Leather

The richness of top grain saddle leather. Extension zip-top. Coin purse on elastic cord. Rayon lined. About 9¼x6 in. Initials sold separately. See below.
88H1816ME—Black   88H1817ME—Red
88H1818ME—Navy   88H1819ME—Saddle tan
Shpg. wt. 1 lb. 2 oz.........Each $6.50

YOURS FOR A BIG WHIRL .. THE FULL CIRCLE SKIRT

Sanforized Washfast Broadcloth in the prettiest prints

Yards and yards of skirt swing out from a tiny waistline for the most flattering fashion of the season. Sturdy Sanforized cotton broadcloth is guaranteed maximum fabric shrinkage of 1% for permanent fit and fullness. So small-priced it's easy to buy both these wonderful skirts . . . teamed with these new-season Honeylane blouses, they'll whirl girls through their smartest summer.

[A] "PRETTY POSIES"—big flower splash all over this whirl-wide skirt. Deep elastic shirred waistline molds your middle, stays put. Skirt is full of flattering gathers below. *State Girls' size* 7, 8, 10, 12, 14. Shpg. wt. 8 oz.
077 H 5101—Colorful floral print . .$1.98

[B] "DANCING DOLLS" . . . newest, gayest print for the big-circle skirt with sleek waistline, side zipper. Bright red braid belt trimmed with clever sewing spools ties in front bow. *State Girls' size* 7, 8, 10, 12, 14. Shpg. wt. 8 oz.
077 H 5100—Multicolor print $2.79

HONEYLANE SKIRTS
Sizes 7 to 14

[A] $1.98   [B] $2.79

HONEYLANE
THE RIGHT WAY TO SAY
GIRLS' WEAR

Sanforized Blouse-Slip	Starchy Embossed Cotton Skirt	Crease-resistant Rayon Check	Sanforized Cotton Cord Stripe
$1.98	**$2.79**	**$2.98**	**$2.98**

Cotton broadcloth, max. fab. shrink. 1% combines pretty back-button blouse with ruffled slip. Eyelet embroidered yoke. Collar, self ruffle trimmed with red zig-zag stitching and bow. Washfast. *State Girls' size* 7, 8, 10, 12, 14. Shpg. wt. 8 oz.
077 H 5757— White with red trim .$1.98

Wide white eyelet embroidery inset all around flashes smartly with every step. Back zipper. Washfast. *Girls' sizes* 7, 8, 10, 12, 14. *State size.* Shpg. wt. 7 oz.
077 H 5117—Copen blue $2.79
077 H 5118—Pink 2.79
077 H 5119—Kelly green 2.79

Neat little checks, fashion's pet pattern for a whirling, accordion-pleated skirt. Smooth side zipper placket. Rayon suiting, dry clean. *Girls' sizes* 7, 8, 10, 12, 14. *State size.* Shpg. wt. 15 oz.
077 H 5120—Navy blue and white .$2.98
077 H 5121—Brown and white 2.98

Big-news fashion . . full skirt swoops crisp, wide apron ruffles to the back, tops them with big bustle bow. Washfast, max. fab. shrink. 1%. *State Girls' size* 7, 8, 10, 12, 14. Shpg. wt. 15 oz.
077 H 5128—Red and white stripe . .$2.98
077 H 5129—Green and white stripe. 2.98

Honeysuckle CIRCLE SKIRTS and DRESSES

LOOK! A complete 360° circle makes a glamorous sweep of swirling, twirling skirts that little girls adore—in a new big choice of wonderful dresses and skirts for Sizes 3 to 6x!

— 360°→

THIS IS IT! The biggest selection we've ever offered of these sweeping success styles. They're all top Honeysuckle fashions . . . skillfully made and gaily detailed with all kinds of pretty trimming. Imagine such lavish use of fine cotton at Sears modest prices!

[A] $3.98 Dress

[B] $2.98 Dress

[C] $2.98 Dress

[D] $1.98 Dress

[E] $1.89 Skirt

[F] $1.49 Skirt

[A] CARNIVAL GAY in bright red iced with white! It's our very best full circle skirt dress styled in crispy embossed cotton waffle cloth with lace trimmed white yoke and all around skirt panelling. Pretty detachable posie at the neck. Washfast. *State size 3, 4, 5, 6, 6x.* Wt. 14 oz. Don't wait, order hers now!
29 H 1040—Bright red with white. . $3.98

[B] CANDY STRIPES in bright green and white pique dramatize this smart, full circle skirt frock. The bodice is frosty white embossed cotton waffle cloth . . . with button back elasticized at waist for snug fit. Flap pocket suspended from waist. Washfast. *State size 3, 4, 5, 6, 6x.*
29 H 1037—Brt. green. Wt. 15 oz. . . . $2.98

[C] AIRY DOTTED SWISS makes a charming party frock—so fresh and cool for spring and summer. Full, round collar edged with lace sweetly frames neckline . . pretty flounced skirt billows-out to a sweeping full circle. The dainty flower bouquets on skirt and yoke are detachable. *State size 3, 4, 5, 6, 6x.* Wt. ea. 13 oz.
29 H 1038—Yellow $2.98
29 H 1039—Light blue 2.98

[D] CONFETTI COLORED POLKA DOTS highlight a dress as practical as it is pretty! White bodice top in fine quality 80x80 percale with multicolor dots. Yoke and sweeping full circle skirt in fine quality cotton broadcloth banded with white. Elasticized waist at back. Washfast. *Please state size 3, 4, 5, 6, 6x.*
29 H 1036—Bright rose; Wt. 8 oz. . . $1.98

[E] WHITE rick rack swirls gaily on this full 360° circle skirt in Sanforized cotton broadcloth—fabric won't shrink over 1%. Adjustable suspenders button on in front . . button back placket. 2 pockets. Washfast. *State size 3, 4, 5, 6, 6x.* Shpg. wt. 6 oz. Cotton blouse illustrated with skirt is described (D), page 8.
29 H 4188—Tangerine $1.89
29 H 4189—Caribbean blue (med.). . 1.89

[F] HEART-SHAPED POCKET with ruffles and lace to win the heart of your little girl. Full circle skirt in a charming cotton percale print floats out to a full sweep. Adjustable suspenders button on in front; button back placket. Washable. *State size 3, 4, 5, 6, 6x.* Shpg. wt. 5 oz. Pretty cotton blouse illustrated with skirt is described (C), page 8.
29 H 4187—Assorted prints . . . . Each $1.49

SIZE CHART for Sizes 3-6X					
Order size	3	4	5	6	6x
If height is	34½- 37	37½- 40	40½- 43	43½- 46	46½- 48 in.
If chest is	22	23	24	25	25½ in.
If weight is	29½- 34	34½- 38	38½- 44	44½- 49	49½- 54 lbs.
Dress length	18½	20	21½	23	24½ in.

SKIRT, BLOUSE, SHORTS AND SWEATER

The fashion-new cotton knit sweater successfully teamed with fine Sanforized broadcloth (maximum fabric shrinkage 1%) to make a versatile set for all day-time, play-time wear

It's a complete wardrobe to take you right through the day! Combine the blouse with the shorts or skirt. The sweater makes a luscious topping for the whole ensemble. THE BLOUSE is a bare-arm style, comes in a delicate floral print on a white ground, has a becoming Peter Pan collar. THE SKIRT is in a matching print, wondrously full; has four belt loops, zipper at side. THE SHORTS come in a matching solid color and feature four belt loops and zipper closing at side. THE SWEATER is a fine cotton knit in matching tone with high-drama bat-wing sleeves. Printed broadcloth bands go down both sides of the sweater. Hand wash sweater separately. "Snag-Pruf" zippers used. A shiny black plastic belt for the outfit is included. Washable cotton broadcloth. Sizes 10, 12, 14, 16, 18, 20. *Please state your correct size.* Shipping weight 1 pound 7 oz.

07 H 6006—Black.....................4-piece wardrobe, boxed $9.77
07 H 6007—Aqua blue................4-piece wardrobe, boxed 9.77
07 H 6008—Rose....................4-piece wardrobe, boxed 9.77

DENIM-LIKE CHAMBRAY BANDANA MATES

Jaunty playwear, sporting draw-strings and bows with touches of red bandana-print cotton broadcloth. Bandana shirt is pre-shrunk, other items are Sanforized, maximum fabric shrinkage 1% .. "Snag-Pruf" zippers.

[F] TAPERED PANTS tie with draw-string on legs. Zipper in back. Washable. *State waistline size 24, 25½, 27, 28½, 30 in. Shpg. wt. 8 oz.*
07 H 5963M—Deep gray.....$2.98

[G] CAPRI-STYLE SHIRT in bandana-print broadcloth. Wear tucked or tied. Washable. *State bust size 30, 32, 34, 36, 38 inches. Shpg. wt. 5 oz.*
07 H 5962M—Red print........$2.98

[H] REVERSIBLE BRA. Wear it with the solid color or print side showing. Washable. *State bust size 30, 32, 34, 36, 38 in. Shpg. wt. 5 oz.*
07 H 5964M—Gray and red..$1.79

[J] SHORTS with bandana-print broadcloth draw-strings. Zipper in back. Washable. *State waistline size 24, 25½, 27, 28½, 30 in. Shpg. wt. 7 oz.*
07 H 5966M—Deep gray........$2.79

[K] FULL SKIRT with 144 inch sweep, draw-string pockets, zipper in back. Washable. *State waistline size 24, 25½, 27, 28½, 30 in. Shpg. wt. 14 oz.*
07 H 5965M—Deep gray with red trim.............................$3.98

NEW! FOR WORK, FOR PLAY, FOR LEISURE

Brand new . . our easy-on wrap-arounds that never gap!

D
Finely
Crinkled
Cotton
$6.98
Sizes
10 to 20;
16½ to 24½

A
No-Iron
Plisse
$3.98
Sizes
10 to 18;
9 to 15

B
Denim
$5.98
Sizes
10 to 20;
16½ to 24½

C
Pinwale
Pique
$4.98
Sizes
10 to 20

A WASHFAST NO-IRON PLISSE COTTON. This lovely new wrap-around easily adjusts to any size bust or waist . . has a scoop neck with gathered front . . full skirt; concealed pockets in side seams. *Misses' sizes* 10, 12, 14, 16, 18; *Juniors' sizes* 9, 11, 13, 15 only. *Order correct size.* Shpg. wt. 1 lb. 6 oz.
031 H 7250—Deep green and white
031 H 7251—Bright red and white
Each. $3.98

D FINELY CRINKLED COTTON . . first time in our catalog . . washfast, sunfast . . won't shrink more than 2% . . needs little ironing . . and a skirt almost 6 yards around! *Misses' sizes* 10, 12, 14, 16, 18, 20; *Shorter Women's sizes* 16½, 18½, 20½, 22½, 24½. Shipping weight 1 pound 9 ounces.
031 H 7258—Multicolor polka dots on white . . .*Order correct size*. $6.98

B DRESS-WEIGHT DENIM . . new and smart this year! A young, pretty back-wrap dress with woven striped trim, flared skirt. Back has V-neck with button. Washable. *Misses' sizes* 10, 12, 14, 16, 18, 20; *Shorter Women's* 16½, 18½, 20½, 22½, 24½. Shipping weight 1 pound 15 ounces.
031 H 7259—Pink with black and white
031 H 7260—Med. blue with red and white stripes. *Order correct size.* Ea. $5.98

E DENIM "CAREFREE" . . Sanforized, won't shrink more than 1%. → Here's a sundress that doubles as a jumper . . looks well with blouses, sweaters. Bodice has securely sewn shoulder straps. Rust-proof brass hook and snap fasteners on the pull-through belt adjust the dress to your own waist size. 6-gore skirt is generously cut for free action; overlaps completely in back. White double stitching for good looks and long wear. Seams finished to prevent raveling; ⅞-inch side-seams for easy altering. Two useful pockets. Wash separately . . as you would jeans. *Misses' sizes* 10, 12, 14, 16, 18, 20; *Juniors' sizes* 9, 11, 13, 15, 17; *Women's* 40, 42. *Order correct size.* Shpg. wt. 1 lb. 15 oz.
031 H 7256—Navy blue. $6.59   031 H 7257—Faded (light) blue. $6.59

C FINE QUALITY PINWALE PIQUE . . cotton that is washfast and sunfast. This back wrap dress is very young and pretty on. White piping . . shirred shoulders with bows . . full skirt. Back has button at neck, 2 at waist. *Misses' sizes* 10, 12, 14, 16, 18, 20. *Order correct size.* Shipping weight 1 pound 8 ounces.
031H7254—Deep blue and white. . $4.98
031H7255—Coral red and white. . . 4.98

E
Sanforized
Denim
"Carefree"
$6.59
Sizes
10 to 20;
9 to 17;
40 and 42

A — Cotton Broadcloth Skirt, Halter and Stole $9.66 complete

B — Cotton Broadcloth Playsuit and Plisse Skirt $7.98 complete

C — Cotton Broadcloth Halter and Skirt $6.98 set

F Denim $2.98

E Terry Knit $2.98

D Striped Seersucker $3.98

SUN-WEAR in bright Sanforized cotton

A Three dramatic parts in a broadcloth printed to look like lovely lace. THE SKIRT is full-flowing, has a zipper closing. THE HALTER is firmly boned. THE STOLE is black fringed, ready to toss over it all. Washable. Maximum fabric shrinkage 1%. *Misses' sizes* 10, 12, 14, 16, 18, 20. *Please be sure to state size.* Shipping weight 1 lb. 12 oz.

07 H 6629—Black
07 H 6630—Rose
Each set........$9.66

B Bloomer-girls are in fashion. And here's a pared-down version. THE PLAYSUIT in broadcloth, full over the hips, with elasticized leg bands. THE SKIRT is multi-stripe cotton plisse, has matching broadcloth waistband with wrap-around sash attached. Washable. Maximum fabric shrinkage 1%. *Please state Misses' size* 10, 12, 14, 16, 18. Shipping weight 1 lb. 8 oz.

07 H 6600—Charcoal gray........Set $7.98

C The popular Indian squaw skirt teams up with a solidtone halter in a festive two-piece set. THE SKIRT is a colorful Indian-type print. It has three fully gathered tiers. THE HALTER zips in back. Both pieces in fine cotton broadcloth. Washable. Maximum fabric shrinkage 1%. *Sizes* 10, 12, 14, 16, 18. *State size.* Shipping weight 1 lb. 6 oz.

07H6627—Aqua blue
07H6628—Red
Each set........$6.98

FUN-LOVING PLAYWEAR for your outdoor life

D SANFORIZED SEERSUCKER sunsuit. Bare-arm style with zipper closing in front. Elasticized cinch belt. Washfast cotton. Max. fabric shrinkage 1%. *Sizes* 10, 12, 14, 16, 18. *State size.* Shipping weight 1 pound.
07 H 6621—Red...$3.98
07 H 6622—Gray.. 3.98

E NEW FASHION KNIT TERRY CLOTH with chenille-type stripes. Two-piece style has elastic waist on both blouse and shorts. Washable cotton. *Misses' sizes* 10, 12, 14, 16, 18. *State size.* Shipping weight 14 ounces.
07 H 6625—Red... $2.98
07 H 6626—Dk. blue 2.98

F SANFORIZED DENIM 1-piece princess sunsuit, white cotton pique trim. Wash separately. Max. fabric shrinkage 1%. *State size* 10, 12, 14, 16, 18. Shpg. wt. 13 oz.
07H6632—Coral red
07H6633—Charcoal gray
07H6634—Faded blue
Each..........$2.98

POPLIN JACKET

Designed for all-purpose, all-weather wear
Fine cotton poplin that's water-repellent
Top-notch tailoring at a value price

Sanforized, max. fabric shrink. 1%. Wash separately. About 25 in. long. Unlined.
Misses' sizes 10, 12, 14, 16, 18, 20. *State size.* Shpg. wt. 12 oz.
7 H 1232—Navy blue
7 H 1233—Bright red
7 H 1234—Dark green
Each.......... $3.98
Women's sizes 40, 42, 44, 46. *State size.* Shpg. wt. 14 oz.
7 H 1241—Navy blue
7 H 1242—Dark green
Each.......... $4.59

- Full-length beaded zipper
- Waistband in back
- Two deep slash pockets
- Adjustable slide buckles

$3⁹⁸
Misses' Sizes

$4⁵⁹
Women's Sizes

NEW SERVICE
This Jacket is now shipped from your Sears Mail Order House

PRIZED LEATHERS

Soft suede and supple capeskin, imported from New Zealand

CHOICE
$26.98
each, cash $3.00 down, $5 monthly on Easy Terms

A CAPESKIN JACKET about 26 inches long. Self belt. Rayon lined. Dry clean. *State size* 10, 12, 14, 16, 18, 20. Shipping weight 2 lbs. 3 oz.
07 H 1203—White
07 H 1204—Bright blue
07 H 1205—Coffee tan
Each.......... $26.98

B SUEDE JACKET, yoke in back. About 26 inches long. Rayon lined. Dry clean. *State size* 10, 12, 14, 16, 18, 20. Shipping weight 2 lbs.
07 H 1235—Copper rust
07 H 1236—Peacock blue
07 H 1237—Taffy beige
Each.......... $26.98

Leather Vest

C SUEDE VEST, handsomely styled with self-covered buttons. Rayon lining. Dry clean. *State bust size* 30, 32, 34, 36, 38 in. Shpg. wt. 1 lb. 12 oz.
07 H 1346—Rust brown
07 H 1347—Dark green
Each.......... $8.95

Vest
$8.95

See our Maternity Sportswear on preceding pages.

Corduroy
$5.98

Denim
$3.98

Gabardine
$7.98

NEW-FASHION JACKETS

Four wonderful ways to turn any skirt into an ensemble

D RAYON, ACETATE AND NYLON GABARDINE. About 24 in. long. Unlined. Dry clean. *Misses' sizes* 10, 12, 14, 16, 18; *Women's* 38, 40, 42, 44. Shpg. wt. 1 lb. 8 oz.
07 H 1340—Navy blue. *State size....* $7.98
07 H 1341—Beige. *State size.* 7.98
07 H 1342—Bright red. *State size....* 7.98

E CORDUROY ZIPPER JACKET, pointed cuffs. About 24 in. long. Wash separately. Unlined cotton. *State size* 10, 12, 14, 16, 18, 20. Shpg. wt. 1 lb. 1 oz.
07 H 1343—Bright red.......... $5.98
07 H 1344—Turquoise green. 5.98
07 H 1345—Medium gray.......... 5.98

F STRIPED DENIM BLAZER-TYPE JACKET with double-fabric notched collar, three smart patch pockets. About 24 in. long. Unlined. Sanforized, max. fabric shrinkage 1%. Wash separately. *State size* 10, 12, 14, 16, 18, 20. Shpg. wt. 14 oz.
7 H 1400—Multicolor stripes.......... $3.98

G DENIM ZIPPER JACKET with rib-knit cuffs and waist. About 24 inches long. Sanforized, max. fabric shrinkage 1%. Wash separately. Unlined. *State size* 10, 12, 14, 16, 18, 20. Shpg. wt. 1 lb.
7 H 1218—Charcoal gray.......... $2.98
7 H 1219—Faded blue.......... 2.98

Value and Style
Zip-front
Denim Jacket
$2.98

NEW SERVICE. Jackets **F** and **G** are now shipped from your Sears Mail Order House.

MIRACLE FABRICS..

Here are the newest and finest, tested by our laboratory, beautifully made into dresses that are miracles of elegance and economy . . they

- wash easily
- dry quickly
- need little or no ironing
- won't shrink more than 2%
- resist wrinkles, rips, mildew
- retain good fit and new look

NEW NYLON SHEER with woven stripes of cotton . . a beautiful fabric in a beautiful dress. Bodice shirring gives you a flattering bustline; V-neckline in front and back, grosgrain trim. Unpressed pleats all around skirt; 2-in. hem. Hand wash. *Juniors' sizes* 9, 11, 13, 15, 17. Shpg. wt. 1 lb. 2 oz.
031H2000—Aqua blue and white
031H2001—Petal pink and white
Order correct size. . . .Each $11.98 →

NYLON with
Cotton Stripes.
$11.98
Sizes
9 to 17 only

40% NYLON
60% Pima Cotton
$9.98
Sizes 9 to 17;
10 to 18

↑ 40% NYLON, 60% PIMA COTTON . . very smart fabric with a beautiful permanent luster. Wonderful new coat dress to wear everywhere, every season of the year. Detachable overcollar and dickey are crisp white cotton pique; skirt has gathers all around. Hand wash. *Juniors' sizes* 9, 11, 13, 15, 17; *also Misses' sizes* 10, 12, 14, 16, 18. *Measure; order correct size.* Shpg. wt. 1 lb. 8 oz.
031 H 2005—Navy blue. $9.98
031 H 2006—Charcoal gray. 9.98

MIRACLE DRESSES

100% NYLON
$7.69
Sizes 9 to 17;
10 to 18

100% NYLON
$7.98
Sizes 9 to 17;
10 to 18

100% NYLON
$9.98
Sizes 9 to 17
only

100% NYLON . . beautiful new semi-sheer with narrow woven "ribbon" pucker . . crisp and billowy. Flattering scoop neckline in front and back with matching jewel-like ornaments; full skirt with gathers all around, 2-inch taped hem. Wonderfully pretty, practical dress . . and it looks very expensive! Hand wash. *Juniors' sizes* 9, 11, 13, 15, 17; *Misses' sizes* 10, 12, 14, 16, 18. *Measure and be sure to order correct size.* Shpg. wt. 1 lb. 1 oz.
031 H 2003—Turquoise blue $7.69
031 H 2004—Coral pink 7.69

100% NYLON . . crisp, very finely crinkled sheer with big polka dots. This dress is wonderfully flattering to a young figure. Pointed bodice gives you a very becoming bustline; the full dirndl skirt accents your slim waistline. Fabric loops and glittering buttons open to below waistline. Hand wash. *Juniors' sizes* 9, 11, 13, 15, 17; *Misses'* 10, 12, 14, 16, 18. *Order correct size.* Shpg. wt. 1 lb. 1 oz.
031 H 2007—Navy blue dots on white $7.98
031 H 2008—Lipstick red dots on white 7.98
031 H 2009—Cocoa (med.) brown dots on white 7.98

100% NYLON . . wonderful puckered taffeta that washes and stays crisp! This is the sheath dress that's extremely smart . . and very easy to wear. Skirt has front pockets, small unpressed pleats each side of back to insure easy fit; 2-inch hem. Piping and bows on bodice are fine quality rayon satin. Fabric belt has rhinestone buckle. Hand wash. *Juniors' sizes* 9, 11, 13, 15, 17 only. *Measure; order correct size.* Shipping wt. 1 lb. 2 oz.
031 H 2010—Black $9.98
031 H 2011—Navy blue 9.98

NYLON REINFORCED GABARDINE SUITS
for
Sister and
Brother

Handsome
Dress-ups
any
Season

A B
$598

C D
3-piece suit
$3.98

Linen-like texture rayon

E F
2-piece set
$1.94
Set in lots of 2 sets

Cool plisse

G
$3.98

Flannel-like textured blended fabric

H
$2.98

J
$2.49

K
$1.94
Set in lots of 2 sets

L
$1.94
Set in lots of 2 sets

New nubby weave!

WELL SUITED for Summer!
Cookie-crowd classics for Easter and long after
In handsome fabrics that need a minimum of care

SUITS for Sister, Brother Steal the Spotlight

A B **LOOK-ALIKE SUITS** of 85% rayon, 15% nylon gabardine. Washable. 3 patch pockets on Eton Jacket. Chest pocket sports its own handkerchief. Boys' longie has elastic waist, detachable suspenders, fly front opening, side pockets. Girls' skirt has pleats front and back, button suspenders, elastic at waist. Sanforized white cotton broadcloth shirts included. *State size 2, 3, 4, 5, 6.* Shpg. wt. suit 1 lb. 4 oz.

BOYS' 3-PIECE SUIT
29H6721—Maroon, gray
29H6722—Navy blue and gray...Suit $5.98

GIRLS' 3-PIECE SUIT
29H6723—Maroon, gray
29H6724—Navy blue, and gray....Suit $5.98

C D **SISTER, BROTHER** look twice as cute in these smart Eton suits of linen-like textured rayon. Washable. Hand loomed embroidered emblem decks the jackets. 2 patch pockets. Boys' boxer shorts have covered elastic waist. Girls' gathered skirt has button-on suspenders. Sanforized white cotton broadcloth shirt included with each suit. *Please be sure to state size 1, 2, 3, 4, 5, or 6.* Shipping weight suit 1 lb.

BOYS' 3-PIECE SUIT
29H6735—Lt. tan, rust
29H6736—White, navy blue.......Suit $3.98

GIRLS' 3-PIECE SUIT
29H6737—Lt. tan, rust
29H6738—White, navy blue.......Suit $3.98

E F **BREEZY COTTON PLISSE SETS** that need no ironing! Shirts have nautical embroidery on pocket. Boys' shorts have covered elastic waist. Bar-tacked front may be opened for fly. Girls' shorts have band front, elastic back waist. Washable. *State size 1, 2, 3, 4, 5, 6.* Shipping weight set 15 oz.

BOYS' SHORT SET
29 H 6557—Red
29 H 6556—Navy blue
Set $1.98; 2 Sets $3.88

GIRLS' SHORT SET
29 H 6559—Red
29 H 6558—Navy blue
Set $1.98; 2 Sets $3.88

MATCHING HAT. *State size 19, 19½, 20, 20½ in.*
29 H 7985—Red, white
29 H 7986—Navy blue, White. Wt. 9 oz....98c

"GROWN-UP" TAILORED SUITS for Little Fellows

G **WASHABLE RAYON GABARDINE SUIT.** Maximum fabric shrinkage 3%. Zipper front jacket. Contrasting yoke, sleeves, trim. Boxer longies with shirred elastic waist, fly front opening, neat cuffs. *State size 1, 2, 3, 4.* Shpg. wt. 1 lb.
29 H 6709—Brown, tan
29 H 6710—Royal blue, gray......Suit $3.98

H **NEW SLACK SET** in fine flannel-like texture 95% cotton; 5% wool. Washable. Wear the sport shirt in or out. Print front blends with solid color of back and longies. Elastic waist. *State size 2, 3, 4.* Shpg. wt. 1 lb. 9 oz.
29 H 6867—Heather (medium) blue...$2.98
29 H 6868—Heather (medium) green..$2.98

J **2-PIECE SANFORIZED 7-oz. DENIM SET.** White cotton terry cloth trim. Covered elastic waist. Sturdy outfit tough enough for play yet "dress-up" cute. Bar-tacked front seam may be opened for fly. Washfast. *State size 2, 3, 4.*
29 H 6554—Faded blue
29 H 6555—Light brown
Shpg. wt. 14 oz...$2.49

K **HEART-WINNING PRINTS** decorate the pockets of a gay cotton gingham shirt. Stripe down sides of cotton poplin shorts match shirt. All around covered elastic waist. Washable. Sanforized—fabric won't shrink over 1%. *State size 1, 2, 3, 4.* Shpg. wt. set 8 oz.
29 H 6418—Red and white.
Set $1.98
2 sets $3.88

L 85% RAYON, 15% ORLON* in a new nubby weave. Washable. Maximum fabric shrinkage 3%. Rib knit white cotton waistband, trim on shirt. All around elastic waist shorts. *State size 2, 3, 4.* Shpg. wt. set 6 oz.
29H6564—Med. blue. 29H6565—Tan
2-piece set $1.98   2 sets for $3.88
* Trade Mark (acrylic fiber) E. I. du Pont Co.

Walt Disney Official
DAVY CROCKETT
"KING OF THE WILD FRONTIER"

4-piece Set for Boys or Girls

$498

- Styled just like Davy's buckskins with western fringe and laced neck
- Exciting picture of Davy in bright, long-lasting colors
- Coonskin-style hat of soft, fur-like cotton pile fabric

Thrill your youngsters with an official Walt Disney Davy Crockett suit. Sturdy brown cotton twill with plastic fringe trim and a plastic-laced neck opening. Long-sleeved shirt has a screen print of Davy Crockett in gay colors. Boys' slacks have elastic waist; girls' skirt comes with an adjustable band. Black plastic belt; brown pile fabric cap. *Please be sure to state size 2, 4, 6 or 6x. Shipping weight 4-piece set 2 lbs. 2 oz. Send your order today.*
29 D 5649—Girls' Outfit . . $4.98
29 D 7377—Boys' Outfit . . 4.98

Walt Disney Productions

MULTICOLOR RED PLAID OVERALL . . . fine pinwale corduroy. Detachable pinafore top—can be worn as separate boxer longie. Full elastic waist for neat fit. One pocket. Washable. *Order today.*
Please be sure to state size 2, 3, 4, 5, 6 or 6x.
29 D 7006—Shpg. wt. 12 oz. $2.98

WASHFAST CRAZY PANTS . . . one-piece; corduroy pants and Sanforized cotton flannel top, trim. *Please be sure to state size. 3, 4, 5, 6, 6x.*
29 D 5832—Red with black and white
29 D 5833—Kelly with black and white
Shpg. wt. 9 oz. . .$2.98

LEOPARD PRINT CRAZY PANTS in washfast corduroy. Elastic-back waist. Ties. *State size 3, 4, 5, 6x.*
29 D 5830—Gold with black leopard print
29 D 5831 — Tangerine with black leopard
Shpg. wt. 8 oz. . . .$1.98

NEW! *Roy Rogers* Coat Sweater

Blue with navy blue design or gray with gold color

sizes 4 to 12 **$194**

SELECT HEAVY COTTON. Firmly knit for warmth. Knitted-in Jacquard design on front and back. Practical button front. Tightly ribbed cuffs and hemmed bottom keep cold out. A sweater that will thrill your boy because all youngsters love to wear Western Clothes! Washable separately. *State color wanted* blue with navy blue design; gray with gold color design. *State size 4, 6, 8, 10, 12. See size chart below.*
43 D 2431—Shpg. wt. 10 oz. $1.94

Western Sweater

NEW! Novel ponyskin design front with durable, knit, sweater-weight cotton back and sleeves. Famous Boyville quality and workmanship. Hand wash separately. Plastic front wipes off, easy to keep clean. Color: brown combination. *State size 4, 6, 8, 10, 12. See size chart below.*
43 D 2440—Shpg. wt. 12 oz. . . $1.89

$1.89

Lambswool and Orlon*

WARM-AS-TOAST 75% LAMBSWOOL AND 25% LONG-WEARING ORLON* SWEATER. So very warm and soft—ideal for all-weather protection. Hand washable. Soft, heather tone Colors blue and tan. *State color wanted. State size 4, 6, 8, 10. See size chart below. Be sure to measure.*
43 D 2250—Shpg. wt. 8 oz. . . .$2.89

$2.89

59c ea. in lots of 2 Short Sleeves

79c ea. in lots of 2 Shirt

$1.94 Hat

Combed Cotton

Striped combed cotton knit shirt. 10% nylon ribbed crew neck. Knit shoulder tape. Wash separately. *State color blue, red, gray. Sizes 4, 6, 8, 10, 12. Chart left.*
SHORT SLEEVES
Shpg. wt. 2, 10 oz.
43 D 4016. . . .2 for $1.18
LONG SLEEVES
Shpg. wt. 2, 12 oz.
43 D 4216. . . .2 for $1.38

Davy Crockett Shirt and Hat

Cotton knit shirt with multicolor screen print of *Davy Crockett*. Soft, interlock knit crew neck. Wash separately. *State color white, pink, maize. State size 4, 6, 8, 10, 12, 14. Wt. ea. 6 oz.*
43 D 4041. . . . .2 for $1.58; Each 85c
DAVY CROCKETT hat of all new coon fur pelts. Leather-like plastic crown. Snap-on tail. Sweatband. Cotton suede-cloth lining. *State Small (6¼, 6⅜); Med. (6½, 6⅝); Large (6¾, 6⅞); Ex. Large (7, 7⅛).*
43 D 784—Shipping weight 14 ounces. . . .$1.94

A $6.98

B $6.98

C $8.98

D $7.98

E $7.29

B
Velveteen
$11.98

C
Orlon and
Wool
$13.59

A
Rayon
Flannel
$6.94

D
Corduroy
8.97
Cotton and
Orlon Jersey
Blouse
$2.97

E
Wool and Nylon
$11.74
Dacron and
Wool Jersey
Blouse
$3.98

THE PRINCESS LOOK

Lovely new silhouette in beautiful
new Kerrybrooke dresses . . especially
flattering to pretty young figures,
especially wonderful in bright red

A **Elegant Velveteen $16.98** . . sizes 7 to 15. Soft, thick-piled cotton with a twill back . . very fine, durable fabric. Flared 8-gore skirt is about 117-in. in sweep . . has wide box pleats all around. Detachable collar and cuffs are heavy white cotton lace. Back zipper to below waist. Fabric belt not shown. Dry clean. Shpg. wt. 3 lbs. *Juniors' sizes 7, 9, 11, 13, 15 only. Order your correct size.*
031 D U1454—Black . . . . $16.98   031 D U1455—Bright red $16.98

B **Our Best Faille $10.98** . . sizes 9 to 17; 10 to 18. Crisp rayon with cotton filling for extra body. Long-line princess dress, brief jacket . . wonderful ensemble! Dress has extra detachable collar of white rayon faille with nailheads; back zipper. Fabric belt included. Collarless jacket has fabric bow, sleeve edging of white rayon faille. Dry clean. Shpg. wt. 3 lbs. *Juniors' sizes 9, 11, 13, 15, 17; Misses' sizes 10, 12, 14, 16, 18. Order correct size.*
031 D U1106—Bright turquoise blue   031 D U1108—Navy blue
031 D U1107—Cherry red   Dress and Jacket . . . . only $10.98

C **Fine Cotton Pinwale Corduroy $8.98** . . sizes 7 to 15; 8 to 16. Velvety soft fabric in a glamorous casual with the new long-line bodice. Full skirt has box pleats all around. Detachable collar is white linen-look rayon. Pearl-like button trim; long back zipper. Dry clean. Shpg. wt. 3 lbs. *Juniors' sizes 7, 9, 11, 13, 15; Misses' sizes 8, 10, 12, 14, 16. Please order correct size.*
031 D U1450—Cherry red   031 D U1452—Gold
031 D U1451—Periwinkle (lilac-blue)   Each . . . . only $8.98

Kerrybrooke

THE <u>RIGHT</u> WAY
TO SAY

FASHIONS

NEW! THE SHIMMERING ELEGANCE OF LUSCIOUS SATIN

The Princess Dress in Softly Lustrous Rayon Satin $16.98 . . sizes 10 to 18. Flattering bodice handsomely ornamented by a Paris-inspired rhinestone buckle. Pretty wide neckline; deep V-neck back. Smooth flowing fullness all around skirt. Underfoundation of acetate taffeta and Pellon® built in. Fabric belt not shown. A wonderful dress, beautifully made in superb quality satin . . fine, close weave . . soft, silk-like luster and texture . . gorgeous colors. Dry clean. Shpg. wt. 4 lbs. *Misses' sizes* 10, 12, 14, 16, 18.

031 **D** U3100—Periwinkle (lilac-blue)   031 **D** U3101—Mint green (light)
031 **D** U3102—Turquoise blue   *Order correct size* . . . . . Each $16.98

The Shirtwaist Dress in Brocaded Satin $14.98 . . sizes 10 to 20. Newest, smartest fashion for dressy daytime wear . . the shirtwaist dress in rich cotton and acetate satin with a raised, self-color woven design. Bracelet-length sleeves with French cuffs and rhinestone-set cuff links. Slim skirt with set-in pockets, 2-gore back, 2-inch hem. A sophisticated, flattering dress, expertly tailored in excellent quality brocaded satin . . firm, closely woven, subtly lustrous, very elegant. Dry clean. Shpg. wt. 3 lbs.
Misses' sizes 10, 12, 14, 16, 18, 20. *Order correct size.*
031DU3103—Mauve pink . . $14.98   031DU3104—Powder (medium) blue . . $14.98

E
Wool
Fleece
$19.96

F
Quilted
Poplin
$9.89

J
Cotton Poplin
Ski-Jacket
$8.84

G
Melton
Cloth
$12.59
Misses' sizes
$13.59
Women's sizes

H
Corduroy
$9.98

K Ski-pants
$6.98 $12.98
Rayon gabardine   Pure wool
with 15% nylon   worsted

color...*adds new*
brilliance to washable
corduroy coordinates

A wardrobe of fashion coordinates in velvety pinwale cotton corduroy . . companion blouses in cotton and jersey to accent the rich colors.

State Misses' size 10 12 14 16 18 20

	10	12	14	16	18	20	
to fit bust	32½	34	35½	37	39	41	in.
to fit waist	24½	25½	27	28½	30½	32½	in.
to fit hips	34	36	38	40	42	44	in.

[A] **Hooded Jacket** . . the new banded hipline. *State size above.* Shpg. wt. 2 lbs.
07 D U6125 — Gold   07 D U6126 — Red
07 D U6127 — Charcoal gray Each $6.74

[B] **Italian-look Slacks,** slickly tapered. Side zipper. *State size above.* Shpg. wt. 1 lb. 5 oz.
07 D 6129 — Avocado green   07 D 6130 — Black
07 D 6131 — Red   Each $4.49

[C] **Shirt-jacket** . . smartly casual. Zip-front. *State size, chart above.* Shpg. wt. 2 lbs.
07 D U6137 — Black   07 D U6138 — Red
07 D U6139 — Peacock blue   Each $3.98

[E] **Toreador Pants** . . print or plain. 2 pockets, back zipper. *Size chart above.* Wt. 15 oz.
07 D 6141 — Print *as shown*   07 D 6143 — Red
07 D 6142 — Charcoal gray   Each $3.87

46 [1955]

A Hercules quilted-lined surcoat of wear-packed selected steerhide . . . expertly tanned to bring out its smooth grained beauty. Soft, pliant, perfectly matched. Fully insulated in body and sleeves with 100% reprocessed wool quilted to high count rayon. 3-piece belt with detachable front sections; back stitched down. Zip cigarette pocket; 2 lower slash pockets. Average length 31 inches. *Please state even chest size 36 to 46 in. Shpg. wt. 6 lbs.*
Reg. Sizes $22.50 cash $2.50 down
41 D U3812—Cordovan (rich, deep) brown....$22.50

For Tall Men. About 2 in. longer in body, 1½ in. longer in sleeves. *State even chest size 38 to 48 in.*
41 D U3813—Deep brown. Shpg. wt. 6 lbs.....$24.75

B Action-free short jacket styling . . . selected steerhide at its supple-tanned best . . . tough and scuff resistant. Warm lining of 70% reprocessed wool, 30% rayon quilted to rayon. Leather facings inside front for longer wear. Collar is double thick leather. Stitched down belt in back; adjustable side straps; side gussets. Average length 25½ in. *State even chest size 36 to 48 in. Shipping weight 5 pounds.*
$19.45 Reg. sizes
41 D U3221—Cordovan (rich, deep) brown. . :.$19.45

For Tall Men. About 2 inches longer in body; 1½ inches longer in sleeves. *Please state even chest size 38 to 48 in. Shipping weight 5 pounds.*
41 D U3228—Cordovan (rich, deep) brown....$21.00

C Hercules quilted-lined A-2 flight jacket with 100% nylon knit waistband and cuffs . . . the finest, longest-wearing knits that could be put on a jacket. Tailored from wear-beating front quarter horsehide—known for its amazing resistance to scuffs . . . hand selected for a perfect match. Insulated with extra warm lining of lustrous rayon quilted over 70% reprocessed wool, 30% rayon. Zip front has protecting overlapping fly; snap fastener neck closure. Collar is double thick leather to hold its shape. Roomy 2-way snap fastened flap pockets with built-in "hand-warmer" slash pockets. Average length 26 in. *State even chest size 36 to 48 in. Shpg. wt. 5 lbs.*
$17.95
41 D U3501—Cordovan (rich, deep) brown....$17.95

Hercules Warmly Lined Leather Jackets and Surcoats

D Hercules B-15 bomber style jacket—with luxurious turn-up collar of dyed mouton processed lamb fur. Streamlined as a 4-engine jet . . . and it's as warm as it is good to look at! Tailored from rich, scuff-resistant top grade front quarter horsehide. Fully lined with 100% reprocessed wool quilted under lustrous rayon. Distinctive yoke front styling with slash pockets smartly concealed in diagonal front welt. Knit waistband and cuffs keep cold air out . . . won't stretch out of shape. Cut over full, roomy sizes for action-free arm and shoulder movement. Average length 26 inches. *Please state even chest size 36 to 46 inches. Shipping weight 5 pounds.*
$21.45 cash $2.50 down
41 D U3561—Cordovan (rich, deep) brown....$21.45

F New Hercules motorcycle jacket . . . a pace-setting two-tone style of black and white selected, scuff-resistant steerhide. Fully lined with sleek, lustrous rayon quilted to an extra warm innerlining of 70% reprocessed wool, 30% rayon. White lapels, epaulets, back shoulder yoke and bi-swing action back. 7-inch zip map pocket, two lower double welt slash pockets, gusseted zipper cuffs—all with smart-looking black and white braided trim. 2-piece belt; chrome-plated buckle. Chrome-plated stud trim. Military shoulder straps. Snap fastened lapels. Average length 23 inches. *Please state even chest size 36 to 46 inches. Shipping weight 5 pounds.*
$24.50 cash $2.50 down
41 D U3227—Black with white trim.........$24.50

E Hercules sheeplined leather surcoat—warmest leather surcoat we sell! Thick, fluffy sheepskin lining for super warmth . . . supple-tanned steerhide for super wear and wind-breaking protection. Large, warm collar of dyed mouton processed lamb fur. Sleeves and 8 inches at bottom of coat lined with 100% reprocessed wool quilted under lustrous rayon. Firmly knit inner wristlets. Zipper front, full length zipper facings inside for greater wear resistance. 2 upper muff pockets; 2 lower flap pockets. 3-piece belt has detachable front sections; back stitched down. Average length 31 inches. *State even chest size 36 to 48 inches. Shipping weight 7 pounds.*
$34.95 cash $3.50 down
41 D U3809—Cordovan (rich, deep) brown....$34.95

G Hercules sheeplined B-15 jacket—our huskiest and warmest bomber style jacket with a thick, fluffy sheepskin lining—like a built-in heater! Tailored from selected top grade steerhide . . . tough, supple tanned, scuff resistant. Sleeves lined with sleek rayon quilted to 100% reprocessed wool. Large turn-up collar of dyed mouton processed lamb fur. Knit wristlets and waistband stop drafts, won't stretch out of shape. Full length zipper pulls all the way up to neck. Corduroy inside facings. Roomy coat-type set-in sleeves. Double welt slash pockets have corded trim. Average length 26 inches. *State even chest size 36 to 46 inches. Shipping weight 6 pounds.*
$26.45 cash $3.00 down
41 D U3563—Cordovan (rich, deep) brown....$26.45

SUB-TEENS . . THIS IS YOUR YEAR!

*Kerry-Teen Coats are Packed with Personality
and You're the Ones to Show Them Off Smartly*

[C]
Wool Fleece, with
Plaid lining
and Scarf
$25.95
cash $3.00 down

[A]
Wool and
Nylon
Car Coat
$17.95

[B]
All Wool
Pinchecks
$24.95
cash, $2.50 down

[D]
Dynel Collar on
Chatham Fleece
$27.95
cash, $3.00 down

[A] BETWEEN-LENGTH SMARTNESS in a fleecy fabric of 75% wool, 25% nylon. Warm interior, too, with lining of 50% wool, 50% alpaca pile on cotton back (face 50% of wt.). Dyed mouton-processed lamb collar, wide storm tab. Some call it the "car coat" some the "suburban look"—but everybody calls it terrific. About 31 in. long. *Sub-Teens' sizes 8S, 10S, 12S, 14S. Please state size.* Shipping weight 4 pounds.
77 G U1640—Bright red; brown fur..$17.95
77 G U1641—Light gray; gray fur... 17.95

[C] HOOT, MON! CLAN PLAID LINING and a fringed head scarf, too . . . making the boy coat smarter than ever. It's Chatham Mills all wool fleece . . back belted, kick pleated and terrific. Red plaid lining and scarf are 45% wool, 55% rayon. Saucer-buttoned for double-breasted look, with big hand-jammer pockets, wide winged convertible collar.
Sub-Teens' sizes 8S, 10S, 12S, 14S. Please state size. Shipping weight 5 pounds.
77 G U1628—Navy blue; red plaid..$25.95
77 G U1629—Camel tan; red plaid.. 25.95

[B] ALL WOOL PINCHECKS with a back view that's worth turning around for. Gores swing out below deep V yoke, with a wide low-placed belt across an inverted pleat. Wing collar, adjustable cuffs. Shank buttons, including an extra for a "spare". Iridescent rayon and acetate taffeta lining, warm reprocessed all wool interlining.
Sub-Teens' sizes 8S, 10S, 12S, 14S. Please state size. Shipping weight 5 pounds.
77 G U1608—Medium gray checks..$24.95
77 G U1609—Beige checks......... 24.95

[D] ALL WOOL FLEECE WITH DYNEL COLLAR. (That luscious Dynel fabric that looks like costly fur). Collar is a soft-rolling wing shape, Dynel on both sides. Coat is Chatham's all wool fleece with deep armholes, tapered push-up sleeves. Hand-piped buttonholes. Iridescent rayon and acetate taffeta lining, all wool interlining. *Sub-Teens' sizes 8S, 10S, 12S, 14S. Please state size.* Shipping weight 5 pounds.
77 GU1604—Cocoa brown; blonde collar.$27.95
77 GU1605—Turquoise blue; gray collar. 27.95
77 GU1606—Rosewood rose; gray collar. 27.95

SWEATERS and SKIRTS

Pair Off in Coordinated Color

E
Felt and
Orlon*
Set
$19.98

F
Orlon Sweater
and
Tweed Skirt
$12.98
Skirt alone
$5.98

G
Orlon Twin
Sweaters and
Flannel Skirt
$15.98
Pullover and
Skirt Set
$10.98

H
Sweater and
Skirt Set
$11.98
Blouse alone
$3.98
Skirt alone
$5.59

*DuPont T.M. for
acrylic fiber

D
$8.98
Set

E
$5.98

F
$7.98

G
$3.98

You're poised and in the height of fashion in warmly hued Sweaters

K
$7.98
Set

H
Was $3.49
$2.98
Sizes 30 to 40

J
$4.98

THIS IS WOOL . .
a leader in casual fashion
*Admirably Suited to
Young America's Taste*

D
Acrilan*
Jersey Blouse
$3.98

Color-keyed
Ensemble . . .
Planned-to-pair

C
Sleeveless
Jacket
$4.98

Jumper
$9.98

B
2-Piece Suit
$19.98

Skirt only
$6.98

A
2-Piece Suit
$26.98
cash, $3 down

TWEED: BEST WITH SUEDE
. . . AND NOW

- Suede resists water stains
- Suede color won't rub off
- Suede can be dry cleaned

E
Acrilan* Jersey
Blouse
$3.98

Tweed Skirt
$8.98

* Acrylic fiber.
Chemstrand T.M.

D
$12.98

E
$12.98

F
$14.98

G
$16.98

OUR PROFESSIONAL UNIFORMS—BETTER 8 WAYS . .

- Miracle fabrics need little or no ironing
- Keep their fit . . maximum fabric shrinkage 2%
- Action-back yokes for freedom of movement
- Seams overcast and double stitched . . can't ravel

- Neat, trim, smooth-fitting narrow waistbands
- 2-inch hems allow for easy alteration
- Fresh-water pearl buttons . . removable shanks
- Choice of ¾ or short sleeves in styles A and B

[A] DACRON* TAFFETA . . long wearing Dacron resists wrinkles and perspiration stains; it's porous, allows your skin to "breathe." This beautiful uniform has a finely tucked bodice yoke; convertible collar, action back yoke; skirt with 3-gore back. 100% Dacron; washable. Shpg. wt. 2 lbs. *Misses' sizes 12, 14, 16, 18, 20; Shorter Women's 16½, 18½, 20½, 22½, 24½. Order correct size.*
¾-length sleeves . . fresh-water pearl button-links, also buttons.
31GU6946—White Dacron..$10.98
Short sleeves . . same style, fabric.
31GU6945—White Dacron..$10.98
*DuPont trademark for polyester fiber

[B] NEW OPAQUE "CRINKLED" DACRON. Dacron is wonderful to wear . . it resists wrinkles and perspiration stains . . it's porous, allows your skin to "breathe" . . and it wears and wears! This handsome new uniform has a wonderful 20-gore skirt that is gracefully flared; shirred action back yoke. All buttons are fresh-water pearl. Permanently crinkled, washable 100% Dacron. Shpg. wt. 2 lbs. *Misses' sizes 10, 12, 14, 16, 18, 20; Shorter Women's 14½, 16½, 18½, 20½, 22½, 24½; Women's 40, 42, 44. Order correct size.*
¾-length sleeves, pointed cuffs.
31GU6939—White Dacron..$11.98
Short sleeves . . same style, fabric.
31GU6940—White Dacron..$11.98

[C] DACRON TAFFETA OR "PUCKERED" NYLON. A smartly tailored uniform with a gathered back yoke and an easy-action skirt with a 3-gore back. Shpg. wt. 2 lbs. *Apron and head band sold separately. . please see below.*

DACRON TAFFETA resists wrinkles, perspiration stains; it's porous, allowing the skin to "breathe." 100% Dacron; washable. *Misses' sizes 10, 12, 14, 16, 18, 20; Shorter Women's sizes 16½, 18½, 20½, 22½, 24½. Order correct size.*
31 G U6933—Light blue.... $7.98
31 G U6934—White 7.98

100% NYLON . . permanently puckered; washfast. *Misses' sizes 10, 12, 14, 16, 18, 20; Shorter Women's 16½, 18½, 20½, 22½, 24½; Women's 40, 42. Order correct size.*
31 G U6912—White $5.98
31 G U6925—Aqua blue.... 5.98
31 G U6935—Pink 5.98

APRON in puckered nylon. Double waistband; ties in back. Washable. *Fits up to uniform size 44.* Wt. 4 oz.
31 G 6949—White.... Each $1.69
Save......order 2 for only 3.20

HEAD BAND in puckered nylon. Double fabric. Washable. Minimum order, 2. Wt. for two, 4 oz.
31 G 6948—White.....2 for 89c
Save......order 4 for only $1.59

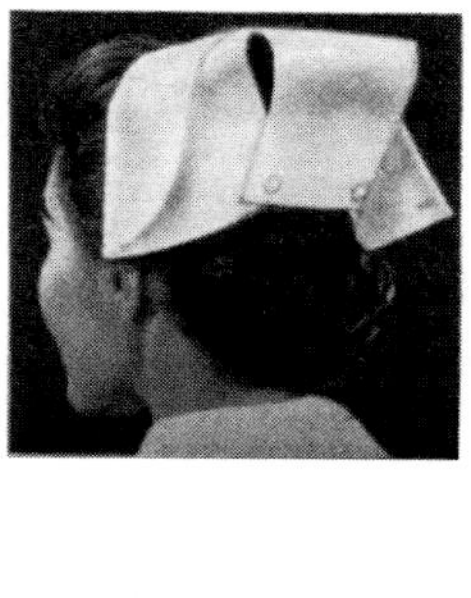

[A]	[B]	[C]	
DACRON TAFFETA	NEW "CRINKLED" DACRON	In DACRON TAFFETA	In PUCKERED NYLON
White only	White only	Light blue or white	White, aqua or pink
Sizes 12 to 20;	Sizes 10 to 20; 14½ to 24½; 40 to 44	Sizes 10 to 20;	Sizes 10 to 20;
16½ to 24½		16½ to 24½	16½ to 24½ ; 40, 42
$10.98	$11.98	$7.98	$5.98
¾ or short sleeves	¾ or short sleeves		

Nylon Head Band 2 for 89c

Nylon Apron $1.69

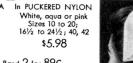

NURSES' CAPS

Permanently starched . . . two-button cap in washable combed cotton, opens flat for easy ironing. Minimum order, 2. Shipping weight for two, 4 oz.
31 G 6917—White
2 for $1.99.....4 for $3.60

FOR MEN AT WORK

HERCULES
REG. U.S. PAT. OFF.

A $5⁷⁵ Herringbone twill   B $5⁴⁵ Blue denim   C $4⁹⁵ Striped denim

D $4⁸⁵ White ducks   E $3⁴⁵ Drill overalls

Reinforced Nation-alls

A TOUGH HERRINGBONE TWILL . . 4 washfast colors. Sanforized 8.5-oz. cotton; won't shrink over 1%. Triple stitched seams; bar-tacking. Bi-swing back. 2 way zip front. Belt stitched down. 8 pockets. *Chest size 34, 36, 38, 40, 42, 44, 46 in. State chest and height.* Shpg. wt. 2 lbs. 9 oz.

51 G 210—Green   51 G 213—Bleached white
51 G 211—Blue   51 G 212—Tan . . Each $5.75

B UNION MADE OF WEAR-BEATING 10-oz. DENIM. Bi-swing back. Removable belt. Fly front; rustproof buttons. Triple stitched; bar-tacked. Sanforized fabric. Wash alone. *Chest sizes 34, 36, 38, 40, 42, 44, 46 in. State chest and height.*

51 G 724—Blue. Shpg. wt. 2 lbs. 13 oz. . . $5.45

C UNION MADE STRIPED DENIM. 2 way zip front. Sanforized fabric; shrinkage 1%. Triple stitched. Wash alone. *Even chest 34 to 48 in. State chest and height.*

51 G 738—Blue/white. Wt. 2 lbs. 13 oz. . . $4.95

FISHER STRIPE TWILL . . as above but 8-oz. cotton, not union made. *State even chest 36 to 46 in., medium length.* Wt. 2 lbs. 9 oz.

51 G 216—Blue and white . . . . Each $4.45

Union-made Work Overalls

D CARPENTERS' OVERALLS . . reinforced to below knee with double layer of tough 10-oz. fabric. New large utility bib pocket. White thread triple stitched seams; bar-tacking. Rust resistant hardware. Sanforized fabric; shrinkage 1%. *Even waist 30 to 44 in.; inseam 30, 32, 34, 36 in. State waist and inseam; tell which is waist.* Shpg. wt. 2 lbs. 15 oz.

51 G 901—Unbleached white duck
51 G 906—Blue and white hickory stripe denims $4.85

ECONOMY OVERALLS. As above but 8.2-oz. boatsail drill with 4 pocket apron. *State sizes as above.*

51 G 900—Unbleached white. Shpg. wt. 2 lbs. 13 oz. . . . $3.85

E SANFORIZED WHITE DRILLS FOR PAINTERS AND PLASTERERS. Rust resistant hardware.

OVERALLS. High back style. Bib pocket opens both sides. 2 brush loops. Double thick suspenders. *Even waists 30 to 46 in.; inseams 30, 32, 34, 36 in. State waist and inseam; tell which is waist.*

51 G 951M—Shipping weight each 2 pounds $3.45

ZIP FLY BANDTOPS. (Inset view). 2 brush loops. 6 pockets. *Even waists 30 to 44 in.; inseams 30, 32, 34, 36 in. State waist and inseam; tell which is waist.*

51 G 960M—Shipping weight 1 pound 5 ounces $2.75

MATCHING JACKET. 5 pockets. *State even chest 34 to 48 in.*

51 G 953M—Shipping weight 1 pound 9 ounces $3.45

[A]
$5.98
Sizes
10 to 18

[B]
$5.98
Sizes
10 to 18

[C]
$6.98
Sizes
10 to 20

[D]
$6.98
Sizes
10 to 18

[E]
Sizes 12 to 20
$9.98
Long Robe
$8.98
Duster

MANY PRETTY LOOKS FOR YOUR LEISURE

Kerrybrooke robes combine smart fashions with versatile fabrics

[A] FLUFFY TERRY CLOTH DUSTER . . your own monogram adds an elegant custom-tailored look! For free monogram in style and color you choose, unbutton collar tab, mail it in addressed envelope enclosed. New half-belt in back. Washfast cotton. Shpg. wt. 3 lbs. *Misses' sizes* 10, 12, 14, 16, 18. *Please order your correct size.*
31 G U8871—White only. $5.98

[C] WASHABLE PINWALE CORDUROY 3-way duster of soft-textured, long-wearing cotton . . with matching fabric tie and binding. Warm, wonderfully comfortable to wear when doing chores at home or lounging. Shpg. wt. 2 lbs. *Misses' sizes* 10, 12, 14, 16, 18, 20. *Please order your correct size.*
31 G U8872—Peacock blue $6.98
31 G U8873—Bright rose. 6.98

[B] PONGEE THAT WASHES . . acetate and cotton that looks like silk; hand wash. New Oriental-style duster with mandarin collar, side slits in skirt. Black cotton piping, "frog" closing. Shpg. wt. 2 lbs. *Misses' sizes* 10, 12, 14, 16, 18. *Order correct size.*
31 G U8869—Ivory with gold and multicolor print. $5.98
31 G U8870—Light blue with gold and multicolor print. $5.98

[D] QUILTED PAISLEY PRINT COTTON with collar and cuffs of deeper-toned cotton corduroy. Short robe has smart side-buttoned closing . . fitted waist, full-flaring skirt. Wash separately. Shpg. wt. 3 lbs. *Misses' sizes* 10, 12, 14, 16, 18. *Order correct size.*
31 G U8867—Med. green on white $6.98
31 G U8868—Med. red on white. . 6.98

[E] ELEGANT EMBOSSED SATIN ROBE OR DUSTER of 100% acetate . . the ultimate in lounging smartness. Fitted waist; wide-swept skirt; long front zipper. Dry clean. *Misses' sizes* 12, 14, 16, 18, 20. *Please measure; order your correct size.*
Full-length Robe. Shpg. wt. 3 lbs.
31 G U7910—Pink on lt. pink. . $9.98
31 G U7911—Blue on lt. blue. . . 9.98

Duster (not shown). Shpg. wt. 2 lbs.
31 G U7912—Pink on lt. pink. . . $8.98
31 G U7913—Blue on lt. blue. . . 8.98

A $2.98
Sizes
12 to 20;
14½ to 24½

B $3.98
Sizes
16½ to 24½;
36 to 44
$4.59
Sizes
46 to 52

C $5.69
Sizes
14½ to 24½;
36 to 44
46 and 48

D $6.98
Sizes
14½ to 24½;
36 to 44;
46 to 52

F →
$6.98
Sizes
14½ to
24½;
36 to 44;
46 to 52

E $6.98
Sizes
14½ to
24½;
36 to 44

Easy-to-wear dresses with longer sleeves

For The GRACIOUS LADY

A WASHABLE 80-SQ. PERCALE coat dress with white embossed cotton trim; 2-gore skirt back. Shpg. wt. 1 lb. *Misses' sizes* 12, 14, 16, 18, 20; *Shorter Women's* 14½, 16½, 18½, 20½, 22½, 24½. *Order correct size.*
31 G U3885—Red print on black
31 G U3886—Gold print on black
31 G U3888—Aqua blue print on medium gray..........Each $2.98

C RAYON CREPE .. glitter buttons. 2-gore skirt back. Hand wash separately. Wt. 2 lbs. *Shorter Women's sizes* 14½, 16½, 18½, 20½, 22½, 24½; *Women's* 36, 38, 40, 42, 44; *also* 46 *and* 48. *Order correct size.*
31 G U5589—Navy blue ground with red and white print.....$5.69
31 G U5590—Dark gray ground with yellow and white print...$5.69
31 G U5591—Copen blue ground with red and white print.....$5.69

E ACETATE AND COTTON PONGEE with pretty print .. has a silk-like luster; hand washes. This becoming dress has shoulder flanges, 2-gore skirt back. Shpg. wt. 2 lbs. *Shorter Women's sizes* 14½, 16½, 18½, 20½, 22½, 24½; *Women's sizes* 36, 38, 40, 42, 44. *Order correct size.*
31 G U3739—Deep blue ground with rose, white and black print...$6.98
31 G U3740—Medium gray ground with yellow, white and black print.......................$6.98

B OUR BEST WASHABLE PERCALE .. tie print step-in dress with white eyelet trim; 2-gore skirt back. Shpg. wt. 2 lbs. *Order correct size.*
Shorter Women's sizes 16½, 18½, 20½, 22½, 24½; *Women's* 36, 38, 40, 42, 44.
31 G U5890—Turquoise blue, pink and white print on black.....$3.98
31 G U5891—Rose taupe, rose and white print on black.........$3.98
Larger Women's sizes 46, 48, 50, 52.
31 G U5892—Turquoise blue, pink and white print on black.....$4.59
31 G U5893—Rose taupe, rose and white print on black.........$4.59

D SEMI-SHEER CREPE .. acetate and rayon for year 'round wear. Duco-print in pink, blue and white. 3-gore skirt back. Dry clean. Shpg. wt. 2 lbs. *Shorter Women's sizes* 14½, 16½, 18½, 20½, 22½, 24½; *Women's* 36, 38, 40, 42, 44; *Larger Women's* 46, 48, 50, 52. *Order correct size.*
31 G U5500—Black ground ...$6.98
31 G U5501—Navy blue ground 6.98

F ACETATE AND RAYON .. year 'round semi-sheer crepe. Lovely step-in dress with white lace trim. 3-gore skirt back. Dry clean. Shpg. wt. 2 lbs. *Shorter Women's sizes* 14½; 16½, 18½, 20½, 22½, 24½; *Women's sizes* 36, 38, 40, 42, 44; *Larger Women's* 46, 48, 50, 52. *Order correct size.*
31 G U3741—Black..........$6.98
31 G U3742—Navy blue......6.98

E
Gingham
Blouse
$2.29

F
Cotton Felt
and Knit Cotton
2 Pieces
$3.98

H
Cotton
Blouse
$2.98

K
Bib-Skirt
$5.98
With Blouse (H)
$8.86

D
Jumper
$4.98
Set
$6.97

J
Skirt
$4.98
With Blouse (H)
$7.86

**Girls' New
FELT FASHIONS**

*with their own blouses
for a go-together look*

**SANFORLAN®
Wool and Nylon**

*They wash, and won't
shrink out of fit*

G
Skirt $3.29
Blouse $1.98
2-Pc. Set
$4.97

L
Jumper
$5.98
With
Blouse (H)
$8.86

M
Acrilan
Jersey
Blouse
$2.98

N
Acrilan
Jersey
Blouse
$2.98

**ACRILAN†
Jersey by Allen**

A

*Light, luxurious,
it washes . .
won't loose shape*

† Chemstrand T.M. for acrylic fiber

P
Honeylane
Boxy Corduroy
$3.98

SWEATER AND SKIRT SETS

Styles D, E *and* F *with high bulk Orlon* tops*
Wear tops and bottoms separately, too.

F
Wool Tweed 'n
Jersey Duet
Set $6.98

D
Jersey Sweater
Sanforlan® Skirt
Set $6.98

E
Sweater and
Corduroy Skirt
Set $5.98

K
Broadcloth
Blouse
$2.19

H
Jumper
$4.98
With
Blouse (K)
$6.97

J
Skirt with Detachable
Suspenders
$3.98
With Blouse (K)
$5.97

QUILTED COTTONS in exciting prints

*Pretty cotton lining
and they wash, too*

CORDUROY
IMP SUIT
G
$4.98

* Dupont T.M.
for acrylic fiber

L
Quilted
and Knit Set $5.98

SUB-TEEN SISTERS
Of the Ivy Leaguers

BACK-BUCKLE SKIRT, BERMUDA SHORTS, LONG PANTS (B, D, F). For you, the adjustable back-buckle, self belt, zipper fly front, slim lines . . . all the mannish features you loved on your ivy league brothers.

These styles and the tops that go with them come in *Sub-Teens'* sizes 8S, 10S, 12S, 14S, 16S. *Please state size.*

A ORLON* TURTLENECK. High bulk jersey knit sweater. Rolled neck. Hand wash. *State size above.* Wt. 15 oz.
77 G 4880—White   77 G 4881—Red
77 G 4882—Peacock blue...Each $3.85
*DuPont T. M. for Acrylic Fiber

B WOOL SKIRT. Front pleat, back buckle. Dry clean. *State size above.*
77 G U5083—Solid dk. charcoal gray
77 G U5084—Solid medium gray
77 G U5085—Copper and gray stripe tweed. Shipping wt. 2 lbs...Each $4.49

C WASHABLE JACKET is 65% Orlon, 35% wool. Flange pleats at shoulders. Unlined. *State size above.* Wt. 2 lbs.
77 G U5086—Royal blue plaid...$7.98
77 G U5087—Red plaid........7.98

D BERMUDA SHORTS, back-buckled. *State size top of page.* Wt. 10 oz.
77 G 5091—Charcoal gray Sanforlan® 85% wool, 15% nylon. Hand wash $3.79
77 G 5092—Black cotton corduroy. Washable....................$2.98

E COTTON CORDUROY JACK-SHIRT. Wash separately. *State size, see top of page.* Wt. 2 lbs.
77 G U5088—Peacock blue.....$3.98
77 G U5089—Red.............3.98
77 G U5090—Black............3.98

F LONG PANTS. Legs taper to ankles with zipper closings, back buckle. *State size, top of page.* Wt. 12 oz.
77 G 5093—Charcoal gray Sanforlan® 85% wool, 15% nylon. Hand wash $4.98
77 G 5096—Black cotton corduroy. Washable....................$3.98

KERRY-TEEN MIXERS
Set and Separates

G TWO-PIECE SKIRT AND BLOUSE SET. Flare skirt is printed washable cotton felt (needs little pressing), has self belt. Cotton knit blouse has matching print collar, trim. Washable. *State Sub-Teen's size 8S, 10S, 12S, 14S, 16S. Shipping wt. 2 lbs.*
77 G U5094—Gold print on black
77 G U5095—Turquoise blue on black
Two-piece set.................$4.98

H FELT FLARE SKIRT. 50% wool and 50% rayon. Deep patch pockets are perked up with buttons and mock buttonhole trim. Wide contrast belt. Dry clean. *Sub-Teens' sizes 8S, 10S, 12S, 14S, 16S. State size. Shpg. wt. 2 lbs.*
77 G U5139—Charcoal gray.....$5.49
77 G U5140—Peacock blue......5.49

J QUILTED SWIRLS OF COLOR dominate this cotton swing skirt. Solid color backing. Plastic belt. Washable. *Sub-Teens' sizes 8S, 10S, 12S, 14S, 16S. State size. Shipping weight 2 lbs.*
77 G U5142—Multicolor stripe..$3.98

K BUCKLED CORDUROY JACKET. Wide wing collar comes to point in back. Buckles on ¾ sleeves, too. Wash separately. Unlined. *State Sub-Teen size 8S, 10S, 12S, 14S, 16S. Shpg. wt. 2 lbs.*
77 G U5143—Peacock blue.....$4.98
77 G U5144—Red.............4.98
77 G U5145—Black............4.98

L COTTON CORDUROY LONG PANTS, slim and tapered. Cuffs and zippers at legs. Washable. *State Sub-Teen's size 8S, 10S, 12S, 14S, 16S. Wt. 12 oz.*
77 G U5146—Black..........$4.29

A $3.85

C $7.98

E $3.98

B $4.49

D Sanforlan® $3.79 Corduroy $2.98

F Sanforlan® $4.98 Corduroy $3.98

H Felt Skirt $5.49

K Corduroy Jacket $4.98

J Lined Quilted Skirt $3.98

G Skirt and Blouse $4.98 Set

L Corduroy Long Pants $4.29

For Sweater See **P**

J Orlon Pullover $4.49

K Orlon Cardigan $5.98

KITTEN-SOFT ORLON* AND WOOL
Easy-Care Skirts . . Hand Washable
Full Fashioned Orlon Sweaters

G Cluster Pleat Skirt $4.98

H Sunburst Pleat. Skirt $5.98

F Corduroy Skirt $4.98

L Corduroy Jumper $5.98

For Sweater See **P**

M Tweed Jumper $6.98 Corduroy $5.98

N Corduroy Skirt $4.69

P Orlon Pullover $3.98

R Hand Washable Skirt and Sweater Set $9.98

*Dupont T.M. for acrylic fiber

C
$29.98
cash, $3 down

D
$29.98
cash, $3 down

E
Without Zip-out Liner
$24.98 cash, $2.50 down

With Wool Zip-out Liner
$29.98 cash, $3 down

C THE NEW PURE 100% VIRGIN WOOL DONEGAL-TYPE TWEED with "brush" surface. More luxurious and colorful with the expensive look of hand-loomed tweed . . properly proportioned for petites. Deep armholes terminate in tapering sleeves that you'll wear pushed up or full length to suit your mood. Rayon and acetate iridescent taffeta lined. 100% reused wool interlining. *Petite Misses' sizes* 8S, 10S, 12S, 14S, 16S, 18S. Size chart on opposite page. *State size.* Shpg. wt. 7 lbs.
17 G U3872—Brown and white mixture. $29.98
17 G U3873—Black and white mixture. 29.98

D IT'S THE LOVELY EMPIRE SILHOUETTE, the fashion theme for fall and winter '56 in 100% virgin wool polished zibeline. It abounds with originality . . in its convertible collar, its stunning double-breasted "bib" front yoke, its high crossed belt in back. Tapering sleeves to wear full length or pushed up. Lined with rayon and acetate iridescent taffeta. All wool interlined. *State Petite Misses' size* 6S, 8S, 10S, 12S, 14S, 16S. Size chart, opposite page. Shpg. wt. 7 lbs.
17GU3868—Medium gray   **17GU3870**–Black
17GU3869–Beige   **17GU3871**–Medium blue
Each.................................$29.98

E WOOL CURL-TEXTURED BOUCLE SURFACE on knit cotton back (face 55%, back 45% of wt.). Scalloped yoke with notched stand-up collar tops ballerina back. Tapering sleeves; fly-away cuffs. *State Petite Misses' size* 8S, 10S, 12S, 14S, 16S, 18S. Size chart, opposite page.
With Iridescent Taffeta Lining of Rayon and Acetate.
100% Reused Wool Interlining. Shipping weight 7 pounds.
17 G U3860—Ivory white   **17 G U3862**—Mauve rose
17 G U3861—Peacock blue   Each............ **$24.98**
With All Wool Zip-Out Liner faced with iridescent taffeta of rayon and acetate to match the coat lining.
17 G U3864—Ivory white   **17 G U3866**—Mauve rose
17 G U3865—Peacock blue   Each, Shpg. wt. 8 lbs. **$29.98**

C

Zip-liner coat
$38.95
cash
$4.00 down
Topcoat only
$31.95
cash
$3.50 down

D

Zip-liner coat
$34.75
cash
$3.50 down
Topcoat only
$27.95
cash
$3.00 down

A

Imported
Cashmere
and
Lambs Wool
Overcoat
$59.50
cash
$6.00 down

B

Zip-liner coat
$39.95
cash
$4.00 down
Topcoat only
$32.50
cash
$3.50 down

Imported
CASHMERE
and
Pure Lambs Wool
THE VELVETY TOUCH OF CASHMERE
COMBINED WITH THE WARMTH
AND WEAR OF LAMBS WOOL
75% WOOL . . . . . 25% CASHMERE

A   C   B   D

looks like silk .. feels like silk .. and washes

First time in our catalog ..
→rayon and silk dresses priced under $12.70
Sale Ends August 17th

$8.00
Each

[A] **Flower Print** . . sizes 10 to 18. An utterly feminine dress with its big bow and full skirt of unpressed pleats. Beautifully detailed in back with deep V neckline, covered button closing to below the waist. Hand wash separately. Shpg. wt. 1 lb. 3 oz.
Misses' sizes 10, 12, 14, 16, 18. Order your correct size.
031 J 5321—Violet, turquoise and olive print on white. $8.00
031 J 5322—Brown, beige and black print on white.... $8.00

[B] **Stripe Print** . . sizes 7 to 15. A wonderful dress, charmingly fashioned with front yoke and fine tucking. Moderately low square neckline in back; full gathered skirt. Back zipper; rhinestone-jeweled buttons. Hand wash separately. Shpg. wt. 1 lb. 3 oz.
Juniors' sizes 7, 9, 11, 13, 15. Order your correct size.
031 J 5008—Peacock blue, white and black stripes. . $8.00
031 J 5009—Bright rose, white and black stripes...... $8.00

[C] **Brush Print** . . sizes 14½ to 24½; 38 to 46. A young-looking dress . . shirred sleeves, shoulder flanges, front midriff, unpressed pleats in front of skirt. Ornament. Hand wash separately. Shpg. wt. 1 lb. 4 oz.
Half sizes 14½, 16½, 18½, 20½, 22½, 24½; Women's 38, 40, 42, 44, 46. Please be sure to order your correct size.
031 J 5753—Lilac and purple print on white......... $8.00
031 J 5754—Aqua and royal blue on white......... $8.00

[D] **Medallion Print** . . sizes 12 to 20; 16½ to 24½. Becoming, well-made coat dress has flared skirt with unpressed front pleats; set-in pockets; rhinestone-jeweled buttons. Hand wash separately. Shpg. wt. 1 lb. 4 oz.
Misses' sizes 12, 14, 16, 18, 20; Half sizes 16½, 18½, 20½, 22½, 24½. Order correct size.
031 J 5327—Olive and gold print on ivory......... $8.00
031 J 5328—Rose and bright copper print on ivory... $8.00

Our Lowest Price Ever!

COOL COTTON and DACRON* DRESSES

A smash hit in this summery lightweight fabric . . laboratory tested to wash, keep its color, resist perspiration stains
SALE ENDS AUGUST 17th

$**7**.**00** Each

[A] **Step-In Shirtwaist** . . sizes 10 to 18; 14½ to 22½. Fly front; silk ascot. Misses' sizes with gathered skirt; Half sizes with easy skirt that has unpressed front pleats, smooth-fitting back. Woven stripes . . washable, needs little ironing. Shpg. wt. 1 lb. 4 oz. *Misses' sizes 10, 12, 14, 16, 18; Half sizes 14½, 16½, 18½, 20½, 22½. Order correct size.*
031 J 3408—Peacock blue and black stripes on white $7.00
031 J 3409—Periwinkle blue and black stripes on white $7.00
031 J 3410—Bright rose and black stripes on white $7.00

[B] **Tucked-Front Dress** . . sizes 7 to 15. A wonderful fashion in soft, pastel colors with dainty bodice detail and pearl-like buttons. The square neckline is repeated in back; the billowy skirt is gathered all around. Long back zipper. Washable. Shipping weight 1 pound 4 ounces. *Juniors' sizes 7, 9, 11, 13, 15. Order your correct size.*
031 J 3269—Light blue
031 J 3270—Light pink
031 J 3271—Light yellow
Each $7.00

[C] **V-Neck Dress** . . sizes 12 to 20. A feminine, full-skirted dress with smart V neckline in back. The silk square pulls through ornament on the belt. Flower print . . washable, needs little ironing. Shpg. wt. 1 lb. 4 oz. *Misses' sizes 12, 14, 16, 18, 20. Order correct size.*
031 J 3414—Turquoise and black print on white $7.00
031 J 3415—Bright rose and black print on white $7.00
031 J 3416—Lilac and black print on white $7.00

[D] **Tab-Trimmed Dress** . . sizes 12 to 20; 14½ to 24½. Well made, youthful dress has hip pocket detail, slim skirt with back kick pleat, back zipper. White linen-look rayon trim and silk square. Washable. Shpg. wt. 1 lb. 4 oz. *Misses' sizes 12, 14, 16, 18, 20; Half sizes 14½, 16½, 18½, 20½, 22½, 24½. Order correct size.*
031 J 3411—Light blue
031 J 3412—Pale green
031 J 3413—Light lilac
Each $7.00

*DuPont T. M. for polyester fiber

A Swimsuit and Jacket **$5.00**
Was -$5.74-

B NEW! Rhumba Ruffle **$3.77**

C 4-Pc. Ensemble **$7.74**

D
NEW!
2-Pc. Playsuit
$2.80

E Save on 2 Polo Shirts
91c Each **2** for **$1.77**

F NEW! Textured Cotton Knit **$1.77**

G Boat Neck Polo Shirt **$1.13** Was -$1.21-

H 2-Pc. Playsuit **$1.74**

J 2-Pc. Playsuit **$1.74**

SAVE . . buy **2** for **$3.36**

D
Set **$11.00**
Suit Alone
$5.50

E
$6.77

F
$7.74

G $7.74 H $6.77
Swim Suit Jacket

K
$13.70

J
$14.67

**New, Easy-Care
MATERNITY
FASHIONS**

[A] Shirt **$3.77**   [B] Pedal Pushers **$2.83**   [C] 2-Pc. Set **$5.74**   [D] Shirt **$2.83**   [E] Shorts **$2.37**

[F]
$2.83
Blouse-Top

[G]
$2.83
Skirt

Cotton Seersucker means less work while you wait

WOVEN COTTON SEERSUCKER, traditionally loved fabric for summer, fashions the Kerrybrooke Mother-to-be garments on this page. Wonderfully *Washable*, needing *Little Or No Ironing*, these easy-to-wear playclothes will take you through the "waiting days" in cool comfort.

[A] **Smart Man-tailored Shirt** .. features Ivy-league button-down collar and comfortable roll-up sleeves. Inverted back pleat gives fullness. *State usual size* 10, 12, 14, 16, 18, 20. Shipping weight 9 ounces.
07 J 7680—White..............$3.77

[B] **Striped Pedal Pushers** .. 4-button adjustment each side of waistband assures smooth, comfortable fit. *State usual size* 10, 12, 14, 16, 18, 20. Shipping weight 9 ounces.
07 J 7698—Copen blue and white .. $2.83
07 J 7699—Pink and white 2.83

[C] **2-Pc. Bermuda Set.** Washable, crease-resistant cotton broadcloth plaid teams with seersucker for a coordinated twosome you'll wear with other separates, too. 8-button adjustment on shorts; generously cut top. *State usual size* 10, 12, 14, 16, 18. Wt. 14 oz.
07 J 7585—Black, red and green plaid with white top...........$5.74

[D] **Zip-front Striped Shirt** .. easy-on, easy-off blouse-jacket for which you'll find dozens of uses! *State usual size* 10, 12, 14, 16, 18. Shipping weight 7 ounces.
07 J 7683—Copen blue and white.. $2.83
07 J 7684—Pink and white 2.83

[E] **Cool Striped Shorts** .. so delightfully wearable. Waistband adjusts with 4 buttons placed on each side. *State usual size* 10, 12, 14, 16, 18. Shipping weight 7 ounces.
07 J 7696—Copen blue and white.. $2.37
07 J 7697—Pink and white 2.37

Checks are Twice Smart when Skirt and Blouse Separates Double as a Dress

[F] **Checked Blouse-Top** .. button-front closing. *State usual size* 10, 12, 14, 16, 18. Wt. 8 oz.
07 J 7654—Copen blue and white checks........$2.83
07 J 7655—Bright rose and white checks......... 2.83
07 J 7656—Black and white checks............. 2.83

[G] **Checked Skirt** .. 8-button waist adjustment. *State usual size* 10, 12, 14, 16, 18. Wt. 7 oz.
07 J 7657—Copen blue and white checks........$2.83
07 J 7658—Bright rose and white checks......... 2.83
07 J 7659—Black and white checks............. 2.83

Coloray* with Thunderbird Styling!

18 Slack style Broadcloths **$3.70** pr. **3** prs. **$10.99**

19 Broadcloth Coat style **$3.77** pr.

20 Broadcloth Pullover **$3.77** pr.

23 **$3.77**

17 Broadcloth Pajamas **$3.77**

21 Cotton Knit **$4.77**

22 **$3.77**

24 Heavyweight Flannelettes **$3.77**

25 New Novelty Heavyweight **$3.77**

27 Pajama-Robe Set **$9.20**

26 Heavyweight Flannelettes **$4.77**

F $3.77   G $2.83   H $1.87 each   J $2.53 each

Sweet Dreams for Sleepyheads in
Honeysuckle Nightwear

K
$1.87
each

L
$2.27
each

M
$2.27
each

N $2.27   P or R $2.83   S 64c   T 3-pc. set $2.67

Candy Cane Red

... and sassy stripes combine to make nightwear news! In Sanforized cotton flannelette. Washable; maximum shrinkage 1%.

N **Girls' Gown.** Elasticized cuffs. *State size 2, 4, 6 or 6x.*
29 D 3460—Shipping weight each 8 ounces.............$2.27

P or R **Pajamas.** Convertible collar. Bloused sleeves, legs; knit cuffs. Wide elastic waist. *State size 2, 4, 6 or 6x.* Shipping weight 10 ounces.
(P) 29 D 3459—Boys' Style with French fly front.............$2.83
(R) 29 D 3458—Girls' Style................................. 2.83

S **Night Cap.** Goes with (N), (P), or (R). *One size fits from 2 to 6x.*
29 D 3461—Shipping weight each 2 oz......64c each; 2 for **$1.22**

T **Infants' 3-piece Set.** Gripper Fasteners at front and crotch for quick diaper changing. Knit wrists and ankles. Double fabric bootees. Tasselled night cap.
Please state size small (9 months, 18 pounds); large (9–18 months; 19–26 pounds).
29 D 3450—Shipping weight set 7 oz.............3-piece set **$2.67**

Charmode Styles for Summer Fashions

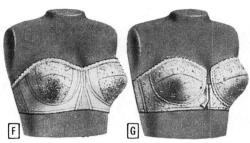

Each $1⁴⁰   Was $2.33 $2¹⁷

Wear these Bras 6 Ways

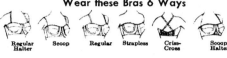

Regular Halter | Scoop | Regular | Strapless | Criss-Cross | Scoop Halter

F **Our Thriftiest Contour Bra** to wear with your bare shoulder dresses. Flattering ¾-cups are permanently shaped with ⅛-in. foam rubber padding to give you a smooth, lovely line. Underwired. Cotton, with embroidered cups. Elastic gore at center front. Cotton and rayon batiste elastic back panels. Back hooks adjust. White. 1-pr. attachable straps included. Shpg. wt. ea. 4 oz.
18 J 3106—Small (A cup). State bust size 32, 34, 36 in.
18 J 4106—Medium (B cup). State bust size 32, 34, 36, 38 in.
Each $1.40 . . . . 2 for $2.56

G **Save 16c on Front Hook Bra** . . so easy to put on. Excellent for wear with plunging necklines as well as with decollette summer styles. ¾-contour cups have ⅛-inch built-in foam rubber padding . . keeps shape permanently . . gives a lovely line. Embroidered cotton front and cups. Underwired cups. Cotton and rayon batiste elastic back. Front band reinforced, hugs bra to you. 1-pr. attachable straps included. White. Shpg. wt. 6 oz.
18 J 3117—Small (A cup). State bust size 32, 34, 36 inches. Was $2.33 . . . . $2.17
18 J 4117—Medium (B cup). State bust size 32, 34, 36, 38 inches. Was $2.33 . . . . $2.17

New Low Bare-back Styles

Bandette $3³³

Exciting low-back strapless style. Embroidered cotton ¾-cups are underwired, have ⅛-inch foam padding for a roundly accentuated cut contour. Batiste elastic side sections . . 1-in. elastic band around back. Back hooks adjust. White. Shipping weight 4 ounces.
18 J 3057—Small (A cup). State bust size 32, 34, 36 in. . . . $3.33
18J4057—Medium (B cup). State bust size 32, 34, 36 in. . . . $3.33

Torso Bra $9⁷⁰

Plunge back to give you glamorous exposure. Works figure magic with fashion's new silhouettes. Front panel and underwired ¾-cups of Dacron* lace, nylon marquisette lined. Airy-light foam in lower bust-cups lifts your curves. Alternate panels of Dacron leno elastic and acetate satin. Coiled wire boning. 4 garters, adjust and detach. White. Shpg. wt. 14 oz.
18 J 4440—Medium (B cup). State bust size 32, 34, 36, 38 inches. $9.70
18 J 5440—Large (C cup). State bust size 32, 34, 36, 38, 40 inches. $9.70

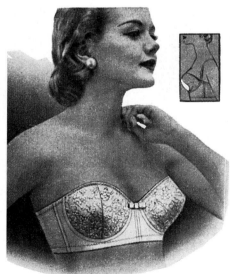

Charmode "Vibrant" Bra

Save 10% $4²⁷
Was $4.77

Sensational "push-up" pads (see small view) heighten and round the bustline to give above-the-bra loveliness. Built-in pad of contoured foam rubber (built to lift, not pad your figure) . . floats bosom up for a high, rounded look. Straps included, wear 3 ways . . with strapless, halter or scoop necklines. Bust-cups are Dacron* lace, framed in nylon taffeta. Dacron leno elastic back panels. Back hooks adjust. *Order an A cup if you are smaller than an A to an average A cup. Order a B cup if you are more than an average A to an average B cup.* White.
18 J 3015—Small (A cup). State bust size 32, 34, 36 inches. Was $4.77. Shpg. wt. 6 oz. $4.27
18 J 4015—Medium (B cup). State bust size 32, 34, 36, 38 inches. Was $4.77. Shpg. wt. 6 oz. $4.27
*Reg. T.M. for DuPont polyester fiber.

Clearance
Save 33% to 60%

Strapless Styles

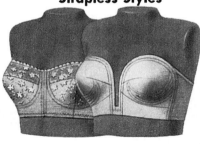

Were $2.97 to $4.97 $1⁹⁷ each

Fabulous clearance of underwired and overwired strapless bras . . timed to the season when you can take the most advantage of this low price as we clear our stock. The styles shown above are only two from this wonderful assortment. Most are cotton and nylon styles with Sears exclusive Cordtex inserts that last the life of the bra and give you firm, permanent support. Some have the Elliptic Cordtex inserts; others the Eclipse Cordtex support. Some are exquisite nylon lace, lined and "cuff-topped" with marquisette. Others are embroidered cotton with ¾-bust-cups that have sheer nylon tops. All are white and have adjustable back hook closing. *Sorry no choice of fabric or style at this low price.* Shipping weight 6 ounces.
18 J 3199—Small (A cup). State bust size 32, 34, 36 inches. $1.97
18 J 4199—Medium (B cup). State bust size 32, 34, 36, 38 inches. $1.97
18 J 5199—Large (C cup). State bust size 34, 36, 38 inches $1.97

Figure Bra Cut 10%

Was $6.70 $5⁹⁷

Figure Bra designed to bring waist-slimming loveliness to the fuller figure. Straps support bust-cups . . no wiring. Hooks conveniently all the way up the front . . so easy to put on. Shaped panels of smooth, firm cotton fabric and Dacron leno elastic sculpture your figure. Boned to give a smoother line. Attractive nylon lace upperbust . . cotton underbust . . lined for support. 4 garters detach and adjust. White. State bust size. Shpg. wt. 10 oz.
18 J 4430—Medium (B cup). Sizes 32, 34, 36, 38, 40 in. . . . $5.97
18 J 5430—Large (C cup). Sizes 34, 36, 38, 40, 42, 44 in. . . $5.97
18 J 6430—Extra Large (D cup). Sizes 34, 36, 38, 40, 42, 44 in. . . $5.97

Torso Bra

Was $4.97 $4⁴⁷ without padding

Foam padded or unpadded underwired cups. Strapless. Shaped bottom. Embroidered ¾-cups, center front. White cotton with cotton and rayon batiste elastic panels. Boned. Back hooks adjust. 4 garters detach. Styles without padding have sheer nylon upperbusts. Wt. 1 lb.

Small (A cup). State bust size 32, 34, 36 in.
18J3404-Without padding.$4.47
18J3407-With padding. . . 4.87
Medium (B cup). State bust size 32, 34, 36, 38 inches.
18J4404-Without padding.$4.47
18J4407-With padding. . . 4.87
Large (C cup). State bust size 32, 34, 36, 38, 40 inches.
18J5404-Without padding.$4.47

Your Robe is Your Companion to Easy Leisure Living

Easy-to-care-for Charmode Quilted Robes and Dusters .. styled to perfection in looks and fabrics .. amply cut to Sears specifications for fine, comfortable fit

F $5.74
Misses' sizes

H $8.71

J $10.76

G $6.77
Misses' sizes

M $9.77

K $8.71
Misses' sizes

L $12.72
Misses' sizes

Back view of Duster N

N $12.72
Misses' sizes

Silhouettes designed to flatter Junior Figures

C $14.70   D $10.74

Charming Bouffant-Skirted Fashions in Rustling Fabrics
.. the new-season look of elegance in line and color

A $8.54   B $10.74

Softer Looking Slim Dresses with New Details

A **Jumper Sheath** in deep-pile twill-back cotton velvet .. so flattering with its wide-scooped neck, front and back. Slim skirt has back kick pleat topped by a neat bow; 2 side seam pockets; back zipper. Wear alone or with blouses. Hand washable. Shpg. wt. 1 lb. 10 oz. *Order correct size. Juniors' sizes 9, 11, 13, 15, 17.*
031 D 5012—Black........$8.54
031 D 5013—Red.......... 8.54

C **Dressmaker Detailed** dress .. tiny dots on soft, lustrous Chromspun acetate taffeta. Empire bodice has deep folds, grosgrain band accents. Billowing skirt with unpressed pleats. Nylon net petticoat. Dry clean. Wt. 1 lb. 12 oz. *Juniors' sizes 7, 9, 11, 13, 15.*
031D7621—Navy; red petticoat
031D7622—Red; red petticoat
031D7623—Amber; brown petticoat
Order correct size....Each $14.70

B **Softened Slim Dress** in fine wool flannel. Wide-scooped neck, front and back; matching rayon satin cummerbund, buckled in back. Tiny pleats give new ease to skirt front. Back zipper, kick pleat. Dry clean. Wt. 1 lb. 8 oz. *Measure: please order correct size. Juniors' sizes 7, 9, 11, 13, 15.*
031 D 6140—Navy blue... $10.74
031 D 6141—Light blue... 10.74
031 D 6142—Lt. jade green 10.74

D **Full-skirted Date Dress** in softly glowing acetate woven with a raised stripe. Jewel-neckline ties in a bow in back. Sleeves have white linen-look rayon trim. Unpressed skirt pleats. Long back zipper. Dry clean. Wt. 1 lb. 8 oz. *Measure; order your correct size. Juniors' sizes 5, 7, 9, 11, 13, 15.*
031 D 6148—Dusty blue with light gray, black and white.....$10.74
031 D 6149—Dusty rose with light gray, black and white.....$10.74

Versatile 2- and 3-piece Kerrybrooke Costumes

5 Clever Ideas for Juniors with a busy schedule . . Office or classroom, dates and dancing!

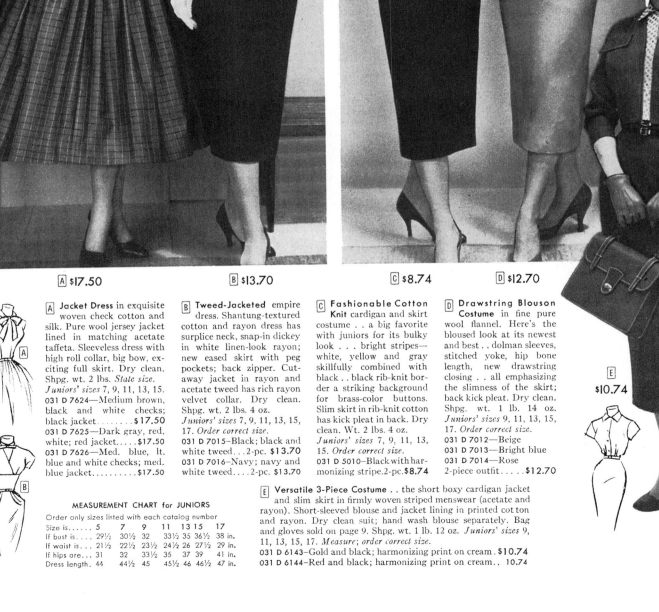

A $17.50   **B** $13.70   **C** $8.74   **D** $12.70

A **Jacket Dress** in exquisite woven check cotton and silk. Pure wool jersey jacket lined in matching acetate taffeta. Sleeveless dress with high roll collar, big bow, exciting full skirt. Dry clean. Shpg. wt. 2 lbs. *State size.* *Juniors' sizes* 7, 9, 11, 13, 15.
031 D 7624—Medium brown, black and white checks; black jacket $17.50
031 D 7625—Dark gray, red, white; red jacket $17.50
031 D 7626—Med. blue, lt. blue and white checks; med. blue jacket $17.50

B **Tweed-Jacketed** empire dress. Shantung-textured cotton and rayon dress has surplice neck, snap-in dickey in white linen-look rayon; new eased skirt with peg pockets; back zipper. Cutaway jacket in rayon and acetate tweed has rich rayon velvet collar. Dry clean. Shpg. wt. 2 lbs. 4 oz.
Juniors' sizes 7, 9, 11, 13, 15, 17. *Order correct size.*
031 D 7015–Black; black and white tweed 2-pc. $13.70
031 D 7016–Navy; navy and white tweed 2-pc. $13.70

C **Fashionable Cotton Knit** cardigan and skirt costume . . a big favorite with juniors for its bulky look . . . bright stripes— white, yellow and gray skillfully combined with black . . black rib-knit border a striking background for brass-color buttons. Slim skirt in rib-knit cotton has kick pleat in back. Dry clean. Wt. 2 lbs. 4 oz.
Juniors' sizes 7, 9, 11, 13, 15. *Order correct size.*
031 D 5010–Black with harmonizing stripe. 2-pc. $8.74

D **Drawstring Blouson Costume** in fine pure wool flannel. Here's the bloused look at its newest and best . . dolman sleeves, stitched yoke, hip bone length, new drawstring closing . . all emphasizing the slimness of the skirt; back kick pleat. Dry clean. Shpg. wt. 1 lb. 14 oz.
Juniors' sizes 9, 11, 13, 15, 17. *Order correct size.*
031 D 7012—Beige
031 D 7013—Bright blue
031 D 7014—Rose
2-piece outfit $12.70

E $10.74

E **Versatile 3-Piece Costume** . . the short boxy cardigan jacket and slim skirt in firmly woven striped menswear (acetate and rayon). Short-sleeved blouse and jacket lining in printed cotton and rayon. Dry clean suit; hand wash blouse separately. Bag and gloves sold on page 9. Shpg. wt. 1 lb. 12 oz. *Juniors' sizes* 9, 11, 13, 15, 17. *Measure; order correct size.*
031 D 6143–Gold and black; harmonizing print on cream. $10.74
031 D 6144–Red and black; harmonizing print on cream. . 10.74

MEASUREMENT CHART for JUNIORS

Order only sizes listed with each catalog number

Size is	5	7	9	11	13	15	17
If bust is	29½	30½	32	33½	35	36½	38 in.
If waist is	21½	22½	23½	24½	26	27½	29 in.
If hips are	31	32	33½	35	37	39	41 in.
Dress length	44	44½	45	45½	46	46½	47 in.

The News.. *Softened Silhouettes*

in fabrics of great elegance

[A] **The Midriff Interest .. in Arnel* Crepe,** a beautifully luminous fabric that looks and feels like precious silk, has a very fine rib. The dress, inclined to the romantic, is completely feminine. Its softly draped surplice bodice is wrapped in a cummerbund-effect of fine pleating; the skirt is a whirl of tiny unpressed pleats. Scoop neckline and long zipper in back; 2-inch hem. Dry clean.
Misses' sizes 8, 10, 12, 14, 16. Shpg. wt. 2 lbs.
031 D 7234—Bright blue   031 D 7235—Black
031 D 7236—Red. *Order correct size...* Each **$14.00**
* Triacetate fiber. T.M. of Celanese Corp.

[B] **The Puff Sleeve Look .. in Lace,** an exquisite Chantilly-type lace in fine nylon and acetate over acetate taffeta. This slim, Empire dress is fashioned for late day and evening. It is sophisticated, yet charmingly soft with engaging details .. a tiny cuff at the front neckline; a flounce at the back of the skirt, accentuated by a huge bow of acetate satin. Square neckline and long zipper in back. Dry clean. *Please measure; order correct size.*
Misses' sizes 8, 10, 12, 14, 16.
031 D 7855—Black   031 D 7856—Beige
Shipping weight 2 pounds.......... Each **$14.50**

[A]
$14.00

[B]
$14.50

The Jewelry . . . Complimentary combination of radiant, simulated pearls and twinkling rhinestones that spells white "after five" bewitchery. 10% Fed. Tax included. Wt. 2 oz.
4 D 4194E—Necklace. Adjusts from 10¼ to 16½ inches via sim. pearl-coupled chain **$4.97**
4 D 4195E—¾-inch clip-back earrings   2.00
4 D 4196E—7⁵⁄₁₆-inch bracelet with rhinestone-studded clasp................. **$3.97**

Elegant Fold-over Clutch in fine rayon faille with rayon satin lining. Handsome gold-color metal frame set with rhinestones. Coin purse. About 9x5½ inches when folded. Price includes 10% Federal Excise Tax. Shipping weight 1 pound.
88 D 382E—Black. Clutch bag........ **$5.26**

The Pump . . New look of soft elegance. The peau de soie (silk) fabric. Gently tapered toe, low cut, foot-slimming side lines, adorable throat bow. Lovely with your dinner dresses. Leather sole, slender high 2¾-inch heel.
Sizes: AA (narrow) width in 7, 7½, 8, 8½, 9.
Sizes: B (medium) in 5, 5½, 6, 6½, 7, 7½, 8.
State size and width. Shpg. wt. 1 lb. 9 oz.
54 D 6151—Black............. Pair **$9.77**

The Beautiful Late Day Dress

Our Finest Cotton Lace over rustling acetate taffeta. A very pretty, young-looking dress with flattering bustline pleats; bow-trimmed bands of taffeta . . big billowing skirt. Scoop neckline and long zipper in back. Dry clean. Shipping weight 2 pounds.
Juniors' sizes 7, 9, 11, 13, 15, 17; Misses' sizes 8, 10, 12, 14, 16, 18. Please measure; order correct size.
031 D 08050—Red
031 D 08051—Light beige
031 D 08052R—Medium copen blue
Each........................$18.50

Billowing Chiffon . . exceptionally fine rayon chiffon with bodice lining and attached petticoat in acetate taffeta. This dress is wonderfully eloquent in its simplicity . . beautifully made with fine tucks in front and back of the bodice; very full gathered skirt; 2-inch hem. Bodice lining is edged with nylon lace. Excellent value! Dry clean. Shipping weight 1 pound 6 ounces.
Measure; order correct size.
Misses' sizes 10, 12, 14, 16, 18.
031 D 7779—Red...........$15.50
031 D 7778—Black...........15.50

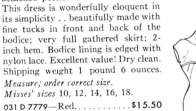

Glittering highlights for romantic fashions. Faceted givree center stones delicately shaded, daintily paired with rhinestones. *State gold-color metal* with pink and rose, champagne and jonquil, or *silver-color metal* with ice blue and blue. 10% Federal Excise Tax included. Shipping weight each 2 ounces.
4D4197ME—Necklace, adj. to 15¼ in. $2.00
4D4198ME—1-in. clip button earrings.. 2.00
4D4199ME—7¼-inch bracelet........ 2.00

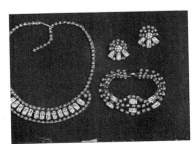

Elegance for After 5:00

Brocade Jacketed Dress . . Skinner's rich, soft rayon and cotton brocade. Jacket is slit in back, bow trimmed; lined in acetate taffeta. Slim, moulded dress with softened bodice . . scoop neckline, zipper. kick pleat in back . . lined bodice; 2-inch hem. Dry clean. Shpg. wt. 2 lbs. *Order correct size.*
Misses' sizes 10, 12, 14, 16, 18.
031 D 8085—Lt. beige...$14.50
031 D 8086—Lt. blue......14.50
031 D 8087—Mauve pink..14.50

Draped Satin Dress . . Skinner's acetate satin fabric with silk-like luster, very fine rib. Softened bodice, accented by a moulded midriff . . full skirt, rounded by unpressed pleats. V neckline and zipper in back; 2-inch hem. Nylon net petticoat; belt. Dry clean. Shpg. wt. 2 lbs. 8 oz.
Misses' sizes 10, 12, 14, 16, 18.
031 D 8095—Royal blue
031 D 8096—Ruby red
031 D 8097—Emerald green
Order correct size. Each. .$17.00

[A] $5.74

[C] $9.97

[D] $7.97

[B] $7.97

[E] $5.97

Fur, Feathers and luxurious textures dramatize the

[A] **Fur-Effect Rayon Plush,** looks like a million, costs so little. Skillfully shaped in the new off-the-face profile line. A fashion success you'll love to wear. Rhinestone ornament. Fits 21¾ to 22½ inches.
Colors white, black, light beige. *Please state color.* Shipping weight 15 ounces.
078 D 3000 . . . . $5.74

[B] **Beaver At A Peak.** Silky beaver fur felt tilted back and rising to smart height. An important fashion point. Bright pheasant feather. Fits head size 21¾ to 22½ inches.
State color fawn (light brown), light gold, ivory white, red or black.
Shipping weight 1 pound.
078 D 3010 . . . . $7.97

[C] **Wide Oval Brim** of genuine beaver fur felt. Folds of rayon satin around the crown, twinkling handmade motifs of gold bullion. A truly elegant dress hat. Fits 21¾ to 22½ inches.
State color ivory white. mauve pink, fawn (light brown) or black. Shipping weight 1 lb. 2 oz.
078 D 3005 . . . . $9.97

[D] **Smartness of Fur.** The full blouse crown is lovely downy rabbit fur. Under it a ripple brim of rayon satin. One red rose for utter gayety . . in fact, the whole effect is one of delightful flattery.
State color white or black. Fits head sizes 21¾ to 22½ inches. Shpg. wt. 14 oz.
078 D 3020 . . . . $7.97

[E] **Glittering Pillbox** of fine beaver fur felt. Softly rounded. A shape smart with everything. Swathed with nylon veiling that glitters prettily with metallic flecks. Fits 21¾ to 22½ inches.
State color black, ivory, white, fawn (light brown), mist blue (light). Shipping weight 10 ounces.
078 D 3015 . . . . $5.97

C Solid color Odyna Topper   D Striped Odyna Short Coat

Our finest fur-like fabric of Orlon* and Dynel

Coats and toppers described below have MILIUM insulated acetate satin
patterned lining for comfort in any weather. Scarf to match included

Same Quality Was ~$99.98~ Last Fall **$79.50** cash, $8 down

[A] **Striped Odyna Coat** shown on opposite page.
Juniors' sizes 7, 9, 11, 13, 15, 17. *Misses'* sizes 8, 10,
12, 14, 16, 18. See charts on page 1510. *Please state
correct size.* Shipping weight 7 pounds.
017 D 2134—Tones of silver gray.............$79.50
017 D 2135—Tones of ranch brown............ 79.50
017 D 2136—Tones of mist gray.............. 79.50

Same Quality Was ~$69.98~ Last Fall **$59.50** cash, $6 down

[B] **Solid Color Odyna Coat** shown on opposite page.
Juniors' sizes 7, 9, 11, 13, 15, 17. *Misses'* sizes 8, 10,
12, 14, 16, 18. Charts on page 1510. *State size.* For
Odyna beret, see below. Shipping weight 7 lbs.
017 D 2137—Blonde beige   017 D 2139—Mist gray
017 D 2138—Platinum gray   (medium)
017 D 2140—Fawn (light brown).............$59.50

Odyna Beret of Orlon and Dynel, smart little muffin,
has rayon grosgrain band and lining. Fits sizes 21¾
to 22½ inches. *Colors* blonde beige, fawn (lt. brown), platinum gray, mist gray (med.) or white. *State color.*
078 D 3900—Shipping weight 9 ounces........$5.97

Same Quality Was ~$59.98~ Last Fall **$49.50** cash, $5 down

[C] **Solid Color Odyna Topper** shown above. Length
about 30 inches. *Juniors'* sizes 7, 9, 11, 13, 15, 17.
Misses' sizes 8, 10, 12, 14, 16, 18. Charts, page 1510.
State size. (See below for Odyna beret.) Shpg. wt. 4 lbs.
017 D 2145—Pearly white   017 D 2147—Blonde beige
017 D 2146—Platinum gray
017 D 2148—Mist gray (medium)........Each $49.50

Same Quality Was ~$89.98~ Last Fall **$69.50** cash, $7 down

[D] **Striped Odyna Short Coat** shown above. Length
about 34 inches. *Juniors'* sizes 7, 9, 11, 13, 15, 17.
Misses' sizes 8, 10, 12, 14, 16, 18. Charts on page 1510.
State size. Shipping weight 5 lbs. 4 oz.
017 D 2149—Tones of silver gray.............$69.50
017 D 2150—Tones of ranch brown 69.50
017 D 2151—Tones of mist gray.............. 69.50

Coats and toppers on these 2 pages shipped from your
Sears Mail Order House. Hat shipped from Chicago or
Philadelphia, whichever is nearer. Order and pay pos-
tage from your Sears Mail Order House. Sears Easy
Terms available. See inside back cover for details.

Our Better Quality Inexpensive Fur-like Orlon* and Dynel

In Solid Color	In Stripes
$47.50 cash	**$64.50** cash
$5 down	$6.50 down

If you have put a ceiling on your budget
and still love rich, fur-like glamour, then
this coat is ideal. Its surface is not quite as
dense or deep as our finest Orlon and
Dynel, but it is choice quality that provides
excellent fashion and warmth. Milium insulated acetate satin lining.
State Misses' size 8, 10, 12, 14, 16, 18.
Chart, page 1510. (See page 16 for hat.)

In New-season Solid Color. Shpg. wt. 6 lbs.
017 D 2141—Platinum gray......$47.50
017 D 2142—Blonde beige....... 47.50

In Rich Stripes. Shpg. wt. 6 lbs.
017 D 2153—Tones of silver gray.. 64.50

* DuPont trademark
for acrylic fibers

F Washable nylon **$5.74**

G Woolen Loden Coat **$9.77**

H Washable Reversible Nylon **$9.77**

J B-9 Parka **$9.77**

K Washable Lined Sateen **$2.83**

L Washable part nylon, part Dacron Jacket **$5.74**

Washable "Gro-Jac" Car Coats
Grow an entire size when you open seams in sleeves and bottom!
Sizes 3 to 6X

M and N Cotton sateen for boys or girls **$8.57**

P 100% Nylon **$9.77**

Open seams in sleeves and bottom for longer wear!

The News is in the Knit Trim

Sheen cotton jackets with fashion's newest touch . . rib-knit trim

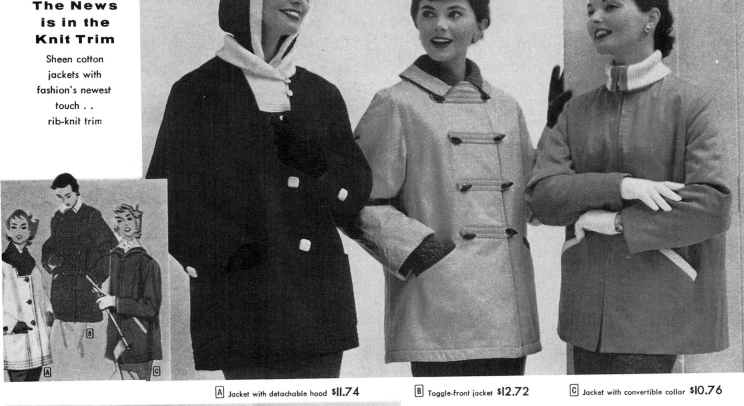

[A] Jacket with detachable hood $11.74   [B] Toggle-front jacket $12.72   [C] Jacket with convertible collar $10.76

↑[D] $14.67
Melton cloth

[E] $12.72
Sheen cotton

Hooded Jackets for winter warmth

Authentic Loden Jacket

in Imported Bavarian Loden Cloth

[F]
$23.97 cash
$2.50 down

IMPORTED BAVARIAN
Lodencloth
WATER REPELLENT
IDEAL PROTECTION AGAINST
RAIN · WIND · COLD

SEARS

Reversible Skirt with Co-ordinate Blouse

G Orlon and wool skirt $2.83 H Acrilan blouse $1.87

Reversible Jumper

J Solid color corduroy jumper reverses to plaid cotton $3.87

Kilty Co-ordinates in Orlon and Rayon

K Kilty skirt $2.67 L Blazer jacket $3.47 M Tapered slacks $2.57
For leotards see page 443 P Hat $1.87 N Dacron-cotton blouse $1.87

Middy Separates in Orlon and Wool

R Acrilan knit blouse $2.57 S Slim-line pleated skirt $2.83
T Tapered slacks $2.83

Sueded Cotton Co-ordinate Sets

V Printed skirt and blouse Set $2.83 W Skirt and check gingham blouslip Set $3.97

Gingham Blouslip

Orlon and Wool Skirt and Twin Sweater Set

Y 3-pc. Set $8.71

Wash 'n' Wear CLASSICS
Luxury Flannel of Orlon and Cotton

A Boy's Style
Blazer Jackets
$7.73

B Girl's Style
Blazer Jackets
$7.73

C Dress
Slacks
$3.97

D Pleated
Skirt
$3.77

E Dress Suit
$11.74

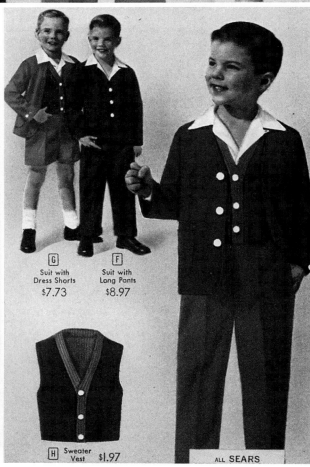

G Suit with
Dress Shorts
$7.73

F Suit with
Long Pants
$8.97

H Sweater
Vest **$1.97**

ALL SEARS

New shapes, Jewel shades

mark the coats of 1958

The High-yoked Coat (above) . . pert, pretty, delightfully young. Its slender lines are fashioned in a soft fabric of 80% wool, 20% nylon, textured with a new homespun-type weave. Adjustable bracelet length sleeves; back walking pleat. Acetate satin lined; 100% reprocessed wool interlined. Wt. 5 lbs. 10 oz.
Misses' sizes 6, 8, 10, 12, 14, 16. Please state size.
T 17 G 2106—Sapphire blue   T 17 G 2107—Red
T 17 G 2108—Black.....$3 down; Each, cash **$29.50**

The Chemise Coat (at left) with the extravagant flattery of a precious mink collar. Pure wool Duvetyn yields its velvet-like texture to the supple freedom of the chemise line . . back fullness deftly narrows toward hem; shapes an exclamation point of newest fashion with a low-placed bow. Tapered sleeves. Lined in acetate and rayon crepe-back satin; pure wool interlining.
Misses' sizes 10, 12, 14, 16, 18, 20. State size.
T 17 G 2539—Ruby red; natural ranch brown mink
T 17 G 2540—Beige; natural ranch brown mink
T 17 G 2541—Black; natural ranch brown mink
Shpg. wt. 5 lbs. 14 oz. . . .$9 down; Each, cash **$88.00**

The Shorter-than-long Coat punctuates its new length with 3 far-spaced buttons .. drapes to an oval back in pure wool polished zibeline. Bracelet sleeves; adjustable cuffs. Acetate satin lined; all wool interlined.
Misses' sizes 8, 10, 12, 14, 16, 18.
State size. Shpg. wt. 5 lbs. 10 oz.
T 17G2611-Ruby red **T** 17G2612-Black
T 17G2613-Star sapphire blue (lt.)
$2.50 down . . . . Each, cash **$24.50**

The Tall Pleated Turban is luxurious rayon velvet, shaped for smartness, comfortable with any style of coat collar. Rhinestone ornaments at front. Fits 21¾ to 22½ in. *State color* ruby red, sapphire medium blue, black, or medium brown.
T 78 G 6715—Shipping weight 13 oz. . **$6.97**

The Oval Silhouette falls beautifully in line with fashion's newest shapes. In rich, deep-textured all wool Worumbo with draped back, low-button front, and new flattering collar. Milium insulated acetate and rayon crepe-back satin lining. Shpg. wt. 4 lbs. 11 oz.
State Misses' size 8, 10, 12, 14, 16, 18.
T 17 G 2125—Sapphire blue
T 17 G 2126—Sand beige
T 17 G 2127—Rose taupe
$5 down . . . . Each, cash **$49.50**

Sheer Pure Silk Organza Scarf has woven stripes in blending colors. About 13x46 in. including self fringe. Hand rolled sides. From Japan. Hand wash separately. Wt. 1 oz.
88 G 8264—Pink to ruby tones **$1.97**
88 G 8265—Star sapphire blue tones . . 1.97
88 G 8266—Gold tones 1.97

The Double-breasted Coat salutes the tapered look in a most important fabric; pure wool, black-looped tweed, richly embered with jewel undertones. Lined in rayon and acetate crepe-back satin; all wool interlined. Shpg. wt. 5 lbs. 12 oz.
State Misses' size 10, 12, 14, 16, 18, 20.
T 17 G 2219—Ruby red and black
T 17 G 2220—Sapphire blue and black
T 17 G 2221—Autumn tan and black
$4 down . . . . Each, cash **$39.50**

Bright Globules of Cabachon stones in rich, Fall colors. Set in gold color metal. Pin, earrings with simulated pearl accents. Pin has safety catch. *10% Fed. Ex. Tax included.*
4G3711E-Dagger pin. 3¾ in. Wt. 2 oz. **$2.97**
4G3713E-Bracelet. 7¼ in. Wt. 2 oz. 2.00
4G3712E-Clip earrings. 1-in. Wt. 2 oz. 2.00

Chemise
. . Trapeze
or simply ease . .
the new shape emerges

Chemise Coat-Dress catches attention with its look of utter ease, its big collar. Back of bodice has bow-trimmed inverted pleat. Dress in shantung-textured rayon, cotton and acetate..fully lined. Dry clean. Pearl bib sold on page 35. Wt. 2 lbs. 2 oz.
Fits Juniors and Misses . . State size 9-10, 11-12, 13-14, 15-16, 17-18.
T 31 G 7206—Coral red.......$14.84
T 31 G 7207—Black........... 14.84

The Glen Plaid Dress .. its story is one of ease, even the fabric, wrinkle-resistant, little-iron Arnel and cotton. Relaxed chemise lines, belted low, ending in a pleated flounce. Convertible collar; 2-inch hem. Hand wash separately: pleats stay. Shpg. wt. 1 lb. 8 oz.
Fits Juniors and Misses . . State size 7-8, 9-10, 11-12, 13-14, 15-16.
T 31 G 6200—Brown and white. .$10.74
T 31 G 6201—Black and white... 10.74

The New Low-belted Chemise Suit, poised, easy, beautiful in fine pure wool .. loops a hip-belt of patent-like plastic. Jacket. about 24 in. long, lined with acetate taffeta. For bag, gloves, jewelry, see respective sections; for hose, page 2. Shpg. wt. 3 lbs. 6 oz.
State Misses' size 10, 12, 14, 16, 18.
T 17 G 9060—Sapphire blue
T 17 G 9061—Autumn green (med.)
$2.50 down........Each, cash $21.50

The Chemise Cloche is of unusually fine wool felt with a soft sheen. Deep crown banded with pleated rayon satin that folds down over the brim in a flat tab. *State color* beige, black, medium sapphire blue, dark brown, white. Fits 21¾ to 22½ in. Shpg. wt. 13 oz.
T 78 G 6720—Hat . . $3.97

A cascade of dripping magnificence . . . in gold color with white pearls. The new lariat style followed through in necklace, bracelet, earrings.
4 G 3730E—26-in. lariat chain. Wt. 2 oz. . . .$4.97
4 G 3731E—Earrings 1½ in. screw back. Wt. 2 oz.$2.00
4 G 3732E—Bracelet. 7½ in. Wt. 2 oz.......$2.97

This is the Trapeze Silhouette! A fascinating new shape with flaring, young lines. Here in a new fine quality Orlon* and rayon plaid . . firmly woven, lightweight, wrinkle resistant. Slightly flared jacket, flared skirt with overlapping box pleats (pleats stay!). Jacket is lined in front and back; skirt has camisole top, long back zipper; 2-inch hem. Dry clean. For shoes, see page 13; jewelry in jewelry section.
Fits Juniors and Misses . . State size 7–8, 9–10, 11–12, 13–14, 15–16. Shipping weight 2 lbs.
T31G7670–Light red and autumn tan plaid **$18.50**
T31G7671–Bright blue and green plaid . 18.50

The New Two-piece Chemise . . shorter top, slimmer skirt. Here in a handsome new viscose rayon and silk tweed with a herringbone weave. Button-back overblouse has leather-look trim. Slim skirt has a wide, shaped waistband; button-trim set-in pockets; back kick pleat; 2-inch taped hem. Dry clean. Flower included. Saucy breton sold in hat section; for gloves, see glove section. For corduroy satchel bag, see page 137. Please measure; *order correct size.*
Misses' sizes 10, 12, 14, 16, 18.
Shipping weight 1 pound 12 ounces.
T31 G 7735 —Black with white tweed . . . **$14.70**

The Chemise adds a Flounce, accents your legs. You'll be irresistable as you swish through the night in rustling acetate taffeta, screen-printed with full-blown roses. The flounce poufs out from a wide, bowed cuff. The collarless neckline dips to a shallow V in back; long back zipper. Dry clean. T-strap shoes sold on page 9. Bracelet sold in jewelry section . . see index. Shipping weight 1 pound 8 ounces.
Fits Juniors and Misses . . State size 7–8, 9–10, 11–12, 13–14, 15–16. Please measure; see green section in back of book.
T31 G 7230 –Red roses on black ground . . **$14.00**

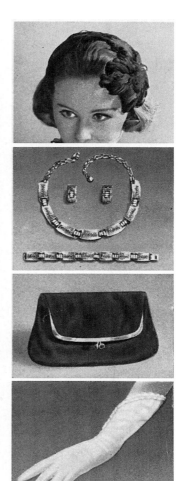

The Bell Silhouette, young and sophisticated, charmingly fashioned in crisp acetate taffeta. Low rounded neckline in back; long back zipper. Pleats and cuff all around skirt; 2-inch hem. The new tapered skirt is wide enough for walking. Dry clean. Jewelry sold in Jewelry Section.
Misses' sizes 10, 12, 14, 16, 18, 20. *State size.* Shpg. wt. 1 lb.
T 31 G 5350—Peacock blue, green, black paisley print..$9.50

The Harem Skirted Dress, curving in and under to accentuate the long-legged look. Here in a winter-blooming print of billowing rayon and acetate taffeta. All-around midriff; acetate velvet belt. Deep V neckline and long zipper in back. Dress is lined from midriff to hem. Dry clean. Shipping weight 1 pound 12 ounces.
Fits Juniors and Misses . . State size 7–8. 9–10, 11–12, 13–14, 15–16.
T 31 G 7203—Autumn gold and brown on black
T 31 G 7204—Sapphire (medium) blue and green on black.........................Each **$13.84**

The Feather Clip is a Siren, all hand-curled feathers and devastating charm. So easy to wear, it clasps your curls with a side-wise curve, fits all head sizes. *State color* sapphire blue (medium), white, red, black, or light pink.
T 78 G 6705—Shpg. wt. 8 oz.**$4.97**

The Elegant Shirred Gloves are long (about 14 in.) double woven nylon with a built-in graceful drape because of the soft shirring. Hand wash separately. *State glove size* 6½, 7, 7½, 8. Shipping weight 3 oz.
88 G 5450—White   88 G 5451—Black
88 G 5452—Sapphire blue (med.) Pair......**$2.83**

Jewelry Tailored splendor. Crystal rhinestone baguettes. Necklace adjusts to 16½ in. ⅞ in. earrings. *State gold or silver color.* Wt. 3 oz.
4G3738E—Necklace, earrings.$4.47
4G3739E—Necklace. Wt. 2 oz. 3.97
4G37?0E—Earrings. Wt. 2 oz. 1.00
4G3741E—Bracelet. Wt. 2 oz. 2.97

Rayon Satin Clutch has a 24K-gold-plated frame. Rayon lining and coin purse. Folded, about 10¼x6 inches. Shpg. wt. 1 lb.
88 G 2629E—Sapphire blue (med.)
88 G 2628E—Ruby red.....$5.26
88 G 2624E—Black........ 5.26
88 G 2630E—Emerald green. 5.26

Rayon Satin T-strap points a tapered toe. Leather sole, 2¾-in. heel. *State size, width.* Wt. 1 lb. 9 oz.
Sizes: AA (narrow) width in 7, 7½, 8, 8½ and 9.
Sizes: B (medium) width 5, 5½, 6, 6½, 7, 7½, 8, 8½, 9.
T 54 G 8395—Ruby red   T 54 G 8396—Black
T 54 G 8397—Sapphire (medium) blue... Pair **$6.77**

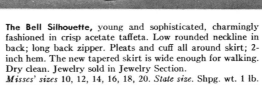

Intimate beginning to your gay
Party Mood

F **Proportioned-length bouffant Petticoat.** 2-tier skirt of embroidered nylon sheer over nylon marquisette. Nylon tricot torso. Elastic waist. *State waist size* 24–26; 27–29; 30–32 in

Short. Fits women 4 feet 10 in. to 5 feet 2 in.
38 G 3093—Pink   38 G 3094—White
Regular. Fits women 5 feet 3 in. to 5 feet 6 in.
38 G 3095—Pink   38 G 3096—White
Tall. Fits women 5 feet 7 in. to 5 feet 9 in.
38 G 3097—Pink   38 G 3098—White
Shipping weight 14 oz................Each **$4.97**

G **The Bra** . . Dacron* and Pima cotton. Gives the high, rounded look. 4-section, circular-stitched cups. Nylon lace uppercups. Elastic at 3-way back hook closure.
State bust size.
Shipping wt. each 4 oz.....Each **$2.83**; 2 for **$5.00**

Color	A-cup. Sizes 32, 34, 36 in.	B-cup. Sizes 32, 34, 36, 38 in	C-cup. Sizes 34, 36, 38, 40 in
Pink	. . . .	.18 G 4751..	.18 G 5751..
White	..18 G 3750..	..18 G 4750..	..18 G 5750..

H **The Panty and Girdle.** Nylon power net with gold color trim. Acetate satin Lastex® yarn back panel on panty. 4 garters. Medium length. See page 282 for white of this style. Pink.
Average Hips, 8 to 10 in. larger than waist. *Waist sizes Small* (24–26); *Medium* (27–28); *Large* (29–30) in. *State waist, hip size.* Wt. 5 oz.
18 G 9110—Panty **$4.77**   18 G 8110—Girdle **$4.77**

J **Royal Purple nylon hose** in delectable jewel colors. Full-fashioned, slim seams. Ultra Sheer. 60 gauge. 15 denier. Shpg. wt. pr. 2 oz. *State color* Ruby red to wear with pink, Autumn gold to wear with white. Also Sapphire blue, Autumn green, Royal shadow (black).
Please state size 8½, 9, 9½, 10, 10½, 11.
75 G 9888—Pair **94c**; 3 pairs **$2.79**; 6 pairs **$5.46**

K **Nylon Power Net Garter Belt** . . light but firm. Gold color trim. 4¼ In. wide at center front. 4 garters adjust. Shpg. wt. ea. 5 oz.
State waist size Small (24–26); *Medium* (27–28); *Large* (29–30); *Extra Large* (31–32) in.
18 G 1737—Pink........Each **$2.34**; 2 for **$4.50**
18 G 1739—White......Each **2.34**; 2 for **4.50**

L **Fashion Garter Belt** of crispy nylon taffeta. Embroidered nylon sheer inserts. Front 6½ in. long. 4 garters. Elastic at back hooks.
State waist size 24, 26, 28, 30 in. Wt. ea. 3 oz.
18 G 1746—Pink   18 G 1742—White
18 G 1745—Blue   18 G 1738—Black
Each..................**$1.40**; Any **2** for **$2.70**

M **Fancy pants.** Nylon tricot brief, embroidered front. Elastic waist, legs. Double fabric crotch. *State color* pink or white. *State size* 30–34; 35–38; 39–40 inch hips.
38 G 5166—Wt. ea. 4 oz...Each **$1.47**; Two **$2.80**
* Reg. T. M. DuPont polyester fiber

The Charming Elegance of Royal Charmode Nightwear

Extravagantly fashioned of luxurious nylon tricot

Ensemble $16.65   Gown alone $7.74

A Drifted over with sheer nylon at peignoir collar, gown bodice. Lavish scalloped nylon lace. Boxed. *State color* sapphire blue, white, champagne (rosy beige). *State size* 32, 34, 36, 38, 40.
38 G 2933—Ensemble. Shpg. wt. 1 lb. 1 oz..........$16.65
38 G 2570—Gown (not available in white). Wt. 10 oz... 7.74

Ensemble $14.67   Gown alone $6.77

B Caressed with hand smocking, lace. Sheer peignoir lit with satin; gown is white sheer over opaque pastel. *State color* pink, lt. blue. *State size* 32, 34, 36, 38.
38 G 2919—Ensemble. (Boxed.) Shpg. wt. 1 lb. 1 oz...$14.67
38 G 2619—Gown alone. (Boxed.) Shpg. wt. 10'oz.... 6.77

Baby Doll Pajama $5.74

C Sweetened with hand smocking, dainty medallions; misted over with white sheer tricot. Dipped in nylon lace. Bloomer panties. Matches ensemble at left. Boxed. *State size* small (32); medium (34-36); large (38) in.
38 G 2959—State color pink, lt. blue. Shpg. wt. 10 oz....$5.74

Pleated Long Gown $11.74

D Exquisitely pleated at front bodice, all around wide sweeping skirt. Touched with hand cut nylon lace at neckline and above ribbon-belted waist. Boxed. *State color* ruby red, sapphire blue. Wt. 1 lb. 1 oz.
38 G 2730—State size 32, 34, 36, 38, 40............$11.74

BEAUTIFUL, DRAMATIC

C
$119.50
Dyed Northern
Back Muskrat

$119.50
Dyed Northern
Flank Muskrat

D
$109.50
Dyed Squirrel

[A] Let-out Natural Mink $599.00   Natural Mink $399.00

Our Finest Natural Mink Stole

[A] The beauty of mink . . perfectly envisioned in this luxurious stole. Let-out pelts of finest quality are matched and tailored with exquisite care. Cape is about 20 inches deep; length of stole from center back to front tip about 33 inches. Rolled collar . . patterned pure silk lining.
State size small (10–12); medium (14–16); large (18–20). Shpg. wt 4 lbs.
T 17 G 0870E—Pastel (medium brown)
T 17 G 0871E—Silver blue (silver-gray)
T 17 G 0872E—Ranch (dark brown)
$60 down, $27 monthly
Total cash price. . . . . . Each $599.00

Prime Quality Split-skin Pelts. Chromspun acetate lining. *State size above.* Shipping weight 4 pounds.
T 17 G 0873E—Silver blue (silver-gray)
T 17 G 0874E—Pastel (medium brown)
T 17 G 0875E—Ranch (dark brown)
$40 down, $17.50 monthly
Total cash price. . . . . . Each $399.00

Natural Norwegian Blue Fox

[B] Fur origin: Norway. The long-maned stole; fashion's newest look of elegance. A silver haze of fur glows from finest grade pelts, drapes the shoulders in a fluid line. Chromspun acetate lining. *State size* small (10–12); medium (14–16); large (18–20).
T 17 G 0876E—Natural (blue-gray)
Shpg. wt. 4 lbs. $15 down, $11 monthly. Total cash price. $149.50

Black-dyed Red Fox. Fur origin: Canada. Chromspun acetate lining. *State size above.* Shipping weight 4 pounds.
T 17 G 0877E—Black . . . $11 down, $9 monthly. Total cash price. . $109.50

Fur prices include 10% Federal Excise Tax

B
$149.50
Natural
Blue Fox

$109.50
Black-dyed
Red Fox

[C] **Dyed Muskrat Sling Cape** . . in a lustrous fur, each pelt perfectly matched and blended. Side cuff-effects; long rolled collar. Novelty chromspun acetate lining. Length about 25 inches.
Misses' sizes 10, 12, 14, 16, 18, 20. *State size.* Shipping weight 4 pounds.
Harvest brown-dyed Northern Back Muskrat.
T 17 G 0879E—Harvest brown (medium)
$12 down, $10 monthly . . Total cash price $119.50
Silver beige-dyed Northern Flank Muskrat.
T 17 G 0880E—Silver beige
$12 down, $10 monthly . . Total cash price $119.50

[D] **Dyed Squirrel Pocket Stole.** (Fur origin: Russia) . . in an important new length, with the regal airs of a framing cowl collar and deep-caped back. Tawny highlights glow from the rich depth of fine, selected pelts. Lined in patterned Chromspun acetate. *State size* small (10–12); medium (14–16); large (18–20). Shpg. wt. 4 lbs.
T 17 G 0878E—Harvest brown (medium)
$11 down, $9 monthly . . . . Total cash price $109.50

In the Evening

the mood is
completely feminine

$15.70 10 to 18 $19.50 10 to 18

Lace and Chiffon in black or red to cast enchantment after 5:00. The dress is wonderfully flattering, beautifully made. Long-sleeved bodice of Chantilly-type lace (nylon, cotton and acetate); billowing skirt of chiffon (acetate and nylon); lining of acetate taffeta. Long back zipper; 3-inch hem. Dry clean. Satin bag, shoes sold on page 9. Shipping weight 1 lb. 4 oz.
Misses' sizes 10, 12, 14, 16, 18.
T 31 G 7747—Black   T 31 G 7748—Ruby red
Order correct size...........Each **$15.70**

Pure Silk Faille, an elegant fabric deftly shaped in a dress of dramatic simplicity. Little buttoned flaps in front . . draped back, bow trimmed. Long back zipper; back walking pleat; 2-inch hem. Finely ribbed pure silk . . dry clean. Feather band sold on page 9. Shipping wt. 1 lb.
Misses' sizes 10, 12, 14, 16, 18.
T 31 G 7742—Black
T 31 G 7743—Sapphire blue (medium)
T 31 G 7744—Emerald green
Order correct size........... Each **$19.50**

The Trapeze Dress shaped in acetate and combed, mercerized cotton faille that looks→ and feels like silk. Full-blown back, rippling with deep inverted pleats, has bow-trimmed, slightly rounded neckline. Front of dress is semi-fitted and lined to keep it smooth. Inner waistband holds dress at waist. Back zipper; 2-inch hem. Dry clean.
Misses' sizes 8, 10, 12, 14, 16. *Order correct size.* Shpg. wt. 1 lb. 12 oz.
T31 G 7753—Coral red T31 G 7754—Med. sage green   T31 G 7755—Black . . . Each **$17.50**

$17.50
8 to 16

92 [1958]

The hand-knit Look

Smartly detailed, new in every way . . the
knit dress that goes everywhere with utter ease!

E
$26.50
10 to 18
New Easy-Care
Estron Acetate
and Nylon Knit

F $19.50 $21.50   G $27.50   H $27.50 $29.50
12 to 20   16½ to 24½   12 to 20   12 to 20   14½ to 24½

PURE CHENILLE WOOL KNITS

A $3.77

B $2.83

C $2.83

D $9.97 Set

E $3.77

F $3.77

G $2.97

H $3.77

J $3.77

Off-beat Plaids

paint the sportswear picture

For leotards,
see hosiery
section

14 SEARS ©ALL

Leaf Patterned Chemise Dress . . new in every detail, including the fabric, 2-ply, Permathal® Everglaze® cotton knit. Softly gathered and bowed in front; buttoned to below waist in back. Boat neckline is perfect for jewelry. Skirt has slits at sides; 2-inch hem. Hand wash. Leather gloves sold on page 13.
Fits Juniors and Misses . . *State size* 7-8, 9-10, 11-12, 13-14, 15-16. Shpg. wt. 1 lb. 2 oz.

 T 31 G 4564—Red and autumn tan. . . .**$7.54**
 T 31 G 4565—Autumn green and blue. . . 7.54

The Hand Crochet Ripple Brim Hat has the perfect casual air for knitted clothes. All wool with puffy popcorn stitch circling around crown. *State color* medium sapphire blue, gold, red, white, black or autumn tan. Fits all head sizes.

 T 78 G 6710—Shipping weight 1 pound. **$4.77**

2-Pc. Chemise Set in fine cotton knit . . high fashion in today's loose-fit silhouette. Over-blouse closes with gold-color buttons. Lined skirt back zips. Hand wash . . Permathal® Everglaze® fabric shrinkage controlled. *State Misses' size* 8, 10, 12, 14, 16. Wt. 1 lb. 6 oz.

 T 7 G 7393—Sapphire blue and black. . . .**$8.97**
 T 7 G 7394—Ruby red and black. 8.97
 Skirt Only. *State size above.* Shpg. wt. 10 oz.
 T 7 G 7395—Sapphire blue, black plaid **$4.77**
 T 7 G 7396—Ruby red and black plaid. . 4.77

The Pure Silk Foulard Square, paisley bordered, has hand rolled edges. About 23¼ inches square, hand washable separately. From Japan. Shpg. wt. 2 oz.
 88 G 8267—Red with aqua and gold. **$1.97**
 88 G 8268—Light blue with autumn tan. 1.97
 88 G 8269—Moss green with autumn tan. . . . 1.97

Sweater "Coat" in Virgin Worsted Wool . . high fashion warmth without weight accented with bulky cable stitching. 2 pockets. About 25 in. long. Hand wash. For scarf, see page 35. *State size* 34, 36, 38, 40. Wt. 1 lb. 10 oz.

 T 7 G 8807—Beige heather. **$15.90**
 T 7 G 8808—Charcoal gray heather. 15.90

Cotton Knit Pants . . completely lined. High-rise waist, back zipper. Hand washable . . shrinkage controlled finish. *State Misses' size* 10, 12, 14, 16, 18. Shgp. wt. 14 oz.

 T 7 G 6452—Lt. brown and autumn copper stripe. .**$4.97**

Tailored perfection in flat snake chain and mesh metal. Necklace adj. to 15¼ in. 1-in. wedding band mesh-like clip earrings. *State gold* or silver color.
 4 G 3724E—Necklace, earring set. Wt. 3 oz. **$3.74**
 4 G 3725E—Bracelet. 7¼ in. Wt. 2 oz. 2.00
 Prices include 10% Federal Excise Tax

F $2.83

G $3.97 Cotton $6.97 Silk

H $2.97

J $3.77

K $2.83 Striped or Solid

L $3.77

M $2.83

N $3.77 Print or Solid

P $2.83 ¾ Sleeves or Short Sleeves

CAPRI PANTS .. the fun fashion of our times
Lean and leggy, they take leisure in their stride

A $5.97   B $4.87   C $4.97

D $2.83   E $2.97   F $3.77

G $4.77 Pants   H $2.83 Pullover

[A] **Stretchable Lastex®** yarn combines with cotton to do wonderful, curve-controlling things for your figure. Back zipper. Hand washable. *State Misses' size* 10, 12, 14, 16, 18. Wt. 13 oz.
T 7 G 6456—Bright blue, green, brown......$5.97

[B] **Fine Cotton Knit** completely lined for shape retention and a smooth sleek fit. Back zipper closing. Hand washable. *Misses' sizes* 10, 12, 14, 16, 18. *State size.* Shipping wt. 13 oz.
T 7 G 6044—Black. $4.87

[C] **Paisley Corduroy** shows a flair for the exótic. Tapered legs slit at side. Back zipper. Hand wash separately. *Misses' sizes* 10, 12, 14, 16, 18. *State size.* Shipping wt. 13 oz.
T 7 G 6454—Red, green and blue print.....$4.97

[D] **Lustrous Sateen ..** fine combed cotton tailored smartly with high-rise waist, self belt, side pocket and side zipper. Washable. *State Misses' size* 10, 12, 14, 16, 18. Wt. 13 oz.
T 7 G 6463—Star sapphire blue.............$2.83
T 7 G 6464—Black... 2.83
T 7 G 6465—Lt. beige 2.83

[E] **Striped Denim ..** sturdy, rugged fabric now more fashionable than ever. Back zipper. Belt included. Washable. *State Misses' size* 10, 12, 14, 16, 18. Wt. 12 oz.
T 7 G 6475—Black, gray and gold stripe....$2.97
T 7 G 6476—Wine red, gray and gold stripe $2.97

[F] **Ribbed Cotton Cord.** An adjustable D-ring waist and slant pockets define a smart look in sportswear. Back zipper closing. Washable. *State Misses' size* 10, 12, 14, 16, 18. Wt. 12 oz.
T 7 G 6470—Ruby red
T 7 G 6471—Black
T 7 G 6472—Deep beige
Each.............$3.77

[G] **Checked Corduroy** pays dividends in fun and fashion. Leather-look belt has gold-color chain and medallion. Side zipper. Hand wash. *State Misses' size* 10, 12, 14, 16, 18. Wt. 11 oz.
T 7 G 6460—Star sapphire blue and black....$4.77
T 7 G 6461—White and black.............$4.77

[H] **Rib-knit Pullover** teams with any and all your pants. Collar nicely shaped; sleeves rolled. Hand washable cotton in cord rib knit. *State size* small (10-12); medium (14-16); large (18). Shpg. wt. 10 oz.
T 7 G 7865—Black. $2.83

fashion points

F $6.77
Black, walnut
or basque red

G $6.77
Black suede or
black calf

H $6.77

J $6.77

K $8.97
Black or
basque red

L $4.77
Black suede
or black
smooth leather

F **A big bold bow** draws attention to this pretty pump. Softly rounded throat and tapered toe. Medium 2⅛-inch heel. Leather sole.
Sizes: AA (narrow) width 7, 7½, 8, 8½ and 9.
Sizes: B (medium) 5, 5½, 6, 6½, 7, 7½, 8, 8½, 9.
Please state size and width. Shpg. wt. 1 lb. 9 oz.
54 G 8373—Black calf..............Pair $6.77
54 G 8375—Walnut (med.) brown calf (B width only)
54 G 8374—Basque (medium) red calf....Pair $6.77

J **Magic Slippers.** Elasticized Spring-O-Lator inside holds to your foot. Deeply etched 2¾-inch heel of flashing Lucite. Leather sole.
Sizes: AA (narrow) width 7, 7½, 8, 8½ and 9.
Sizes: B (medium) 5, 5½, 6, 6½, 7, 7½, 8, 8½, 9.
Please state size and width. Shpg. wt. 1 lb. 9 oz.
54 G 8428—Clear vinyl plastic.........Pair $6.77

G **Alluringly feminine,** designed for dancing. Like delicate lace, tiny vamp cut-outs reveal, conceal a dainty foot. Graceful tapered toe, made over a natural-fitting combination last. Reed-slim 2¾-inch high heel. Leather sole.
Sizes: B (medium) 5, 5½, 6, 6½, 7, 7½, 8, 8½, 9.
Please state size wanted. Shipping wt. 1 lb. 9 oz.
54 G 8444—Black suede...............Pair $6.77
54 G 8445—Black calf.................Pair 6.77

K **Wide cuffed Featherlite.** Combination last. Tapered toe. 2¾-inch heel. Leather sole.
Sizes: AA (narrow) width in 7, 7½, 8, 8½, 9.
Sizes: B (medium) 5, 5½, 6, 6½, 7, 7½, 8, 8½, 9.
Please state size and width. Shpg. wt. 1 lb. 9 oz.
T 54 G 6393—Black calf, gunmetal trim....Pair $8.97
T 54 G 6392—Basque red calf, black trim..Pair 8.97

H **A striking silhouette** with a big loop buckle, cut on same slimming lines as the tapered toe. Combination last hugs your heel. Poised on a medium 2¼-inch heel, artfully shaped to look much higher than it is. Leather sole.
Sizes: AA (narrow) width in 7, 7½, 8, 8½ and 9.
Sizes: B (medium) 5, 5½, 6, 6½, 7, 7½, 8, 8½, 9.
Please state size and width. Shpg. wt. 1 lb. 9 oz.
54 G 8430—Black calf.................Pair $6.77

L **Draped and shaped** to flatter your foot. Round throat pump with tapered toe. High 2¾-inch heel. Guardtex composition sole.
Sizes: C (medium wide) in 5, 5½, 6, 6½, 7, 7½, 8, 8½, 9. *Please state size.* Shpg. wt. 1 lb. 9 oz.
54 G 8418—Black suede...............Pair $4.77
54 G 8419—Black smooth leather........Pair 4.77

M Black suede or
black calf

Dapper by day . . dazzling by night

- Collar down for a trim tailored line
- Collar up for sparkling sophistication

$9.77 PAIR

M Two shoes for the price of one! Wear the collar down to form a neat cuff . . simple footnotes to daytime dresses. Turned up, it exposes a glittering tiara of rhinestones, backed by a regal stand-up throat. All on a frankly flattering Featherlite pump. Fashion's pointed stiletto toe, shaped over the natural-fitting proportioned last. Seated royally on a high slender 2¾-inch heel. Leather sole.
Sizes: AA (narrow) width in 7, 7½, 8, 8½ and 9.
Sizes: B (medium) width in 5, 5½, 6, 6½, 7, 7½, 8, 8½ and 9.
Please be sure to state size and width. Shipping weight 1 lb. 9 oz.
T 54 G 6126—Black suede leather.....................Pair $9.77
T 54 G 6128—Black calfskin.......................Pair 9.77

$12.90 each
Misses' sizes
$14.90 each
Half sizes

Colorful
Cotton Raincoats

Thick 'n' Thin Wale Corduroy, a favorite fabric for rain or shine in poster-paint colors that brighten any weather. The pretty, matching hat and coat are lined in Milium insulated rayon and acetate iridescent taffeta. Water repellent. Wt. 4 lbs. 8 oz.
Misses' sizes 10, 12, 14, 16, 18, 20. *Please state size.*
Ⴀ 17F6545–Bright red....$12.90
Ⴀ 17F6546–Peacock blue.. 12.90
Ⴀ 17F6547–Amber tan.... 12.90
Half sizes 14½, 16½, 18½, 20½, 22½, 24½. *State size.*
Ⴀ 17F6900–Bright red....$14.90
Ⴀ 17F6901–Peacock blue.. 14.90
Ⴀ 17F6902–Amber tan.... 14.90

Textured Tweed . . fashioned with fine exit lines; buttoned back tab, swinging back pleat. Hat and coat lined with rayon and acetate iridescent taffeta. Water repellent.
Misses' sizes 8, 10, 12, 14, 16, 18. *Please state size.*
Ⴀ 17F6578–Black and white
Ⴀ 17F6579–Aqua blue and gray
Ⴀ 17F6580–Mauve pink and gray
Wt. 3 lbs. 11 oz.....Each $12.90
Half sizes 14½, 16½, 18½, 20½, 22½, 24½. *State size.*
Ⴀ 17F6904–Black and white
Ⴀ 17F6905–Aqua blue and gray
Ⴀ 17F6906–Mauve pink and gray
Wt. 3 lbs. 11 oz.....Each $14.90

The Chic Ensemble. A deliberately tailored coat of acetate and rayon flannel; gay umbrella, scarf, hat and coat lining of matching acetate taffeta paisley. Water repellent.
Misses' sizes 10, 12, 14, 16, 18, 20. *State size.* Shpg. wt. 4 lbs. 2 oz.
Ⴀ 17 F 06581–Med. gray; blue print
Ⴀ 17 F 06582–Dk. brown; beige print
Ⴀ 17 F 06583–Dk. oxford blue; blue print. . . $2 down. Each, cash $19.90
$19.90

Textured Cotton Checks the signature of its great designer . . styled with true dash; bold pattern, big pockets, impetuous back flare. Lined for fun in bright red Milium insulated acetate taffeta. Water-repellent for going anywhere.
State Misses' size 8, 10, 12, 14, 16, 18. Shpg. wt. 4 lbs. 2 oz.
Ⴀ 17 F 6577–Black and white
$2.00 down . . . . Cash $19.90
'$19.90

Styled by
Schiaparelli
for Sears

At home Fashions

for hostess or homemaker

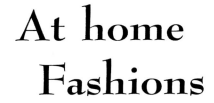

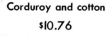

Corduroy and cotton
$10.76

This little outfit stays at home, in beautiful comfort. Paisley print cotton shirt to wear under an adorable coachman vest of corduroy, lined with the print blouse material. Tapered corduroy pants zip up the side. 2 pockets. Washable.
  Color red. State blouse size 32, 34, 36, 38, 40. State pants size 10, 12, 14, 16, 18. Shipping weight 2 lbs. 8 oz.
38 G 9798....3-piece set $10.76

Drip-dry and knit cotton
$9.77

Why go out? . . . not when you can relax in such fashionable ease.   Wrap-style side-zip blouse in playful, posy printed drip-dry cotton. Tapered knit pants in harmonizing solid color; back zipper. Flaring sash. One pocket. Washable.
State blouse size 32, 34, 36, 38, 40; pants size 10, 12, 14, 16, 18.
38 G 9787—Red print, olive green
38 G 9788—Orange print, blue.
Shpg. wt. 2 lbs. . . . .3-pc. set **$9.77**

Cotton sateen, corduroy
$8.71

Glamour takes it easy around the house . . in a fetching, floral printed combed sateen shirt with roll up sleeves. Figure-slimming, tapered corduroy pants zip up the side, have 2 pockets. Washable.
State blouse size 32, 34, 36, 38, 40; pants size 10, 12, 14, 16, 18.
38 G 9796—Aqua blue print, black
38 G 9797—Red print, black
Shipping weight 2 lbs. 2 oz.
2-piece set.............**$8.71**

MISSES' MEASURING CHART FOR 2 AND 3-PIECE LOUNGE SETS										
Chart for Pants							Chart for blouses and shirts			
Size is	10	12	14	16	18	20	Size is	32	34	36	38	40
If waist is	24½	25½	27	28½	30½	32½	If bust is	31–32	33–34	35–36	37–38	39–40
If hips are	34	36	38	40	42	44	Be sure to state two sizes for 2-piece outfits				

3-piece Outfit combines a wool flannel weskit and skirt with a cotton broadcloth blouse. New short length weskit buttons at waist. Slim skirt has a double row of buttons, front kick pleat, side zipper. Both dry clean. Washable, crease-resistant blouse has cuffed sleeves with button links; Sanforized; max. fabric shrink. 1%. For pin, see page 25B.
State Junior's size 7, 9, 11, 13, 15.

T7 F 7133—Dark oxford gray with white blouse. Wt. 1 lb. 2 oz. **$10.94**

Pinwale Corduroy . . princess-styled with a full eight-gore skirt. 2 hip pockets. Back zipper. Hand wash. For blue hose, see hosiery pages. *Junior's sizes 7, 9, 11, 13, 15. State size.* Shipping wt. 1 lb. 3 oz.
T7 F 5872—Copen blue **$5.97**
T7 F 5873—Black 5.97

Gingham Checked Blouse in combed cotton; white pique collar. Hand wash. *State bust size 30, 32, 34, 36, 38.*
T7 F 6795—Blue, white and black Shipping weight 5 oz. **$2.97**

Hi-rise Suspender Skirt in soft wool flannel. Tassel trim. Back zipper. Dry clean. Shipping wt. 1 lb. 4 oz. *State Junior's size 7, 9, 11, 13, 15.*
T7 F 4582—Red **$7.97**
T7 F 4583—Black 7.97

Cotton Broadcloth Blouse . . embroidered sleeves. Washable; drip dry; crease resistant.
State bust size 30, 32, 34, 36, 38.
T7 F 2871—White with red
T7 F 2872—White with black
Shipping weight 11 oz. . Each **$3.94**

2-Pc. 100% Worsted Wool Knit in a beautiful basic dress and jumper-cardigan. Sleeveless cardigan is new and smart, can be worn with other things. The top of the dress is a novelty knit; fine-ribbed, elasticized waist for a neat fit. Dry clean. Suede flatties, and a matching bag, on page 5. Shpg. wt. 1 lb. 8 oz. *State Junior's size 7, 9, 11, 13, 15.*

T31 F 8240—Turquoise **$16.50**
T31 F 8241—Lt. beige. 16.50
T31 F 8242—Bright red 16.50

Stay-in Pleats
wash..drip dry..are
ready to wear

G Set of 2 for $1.97   H $1.97

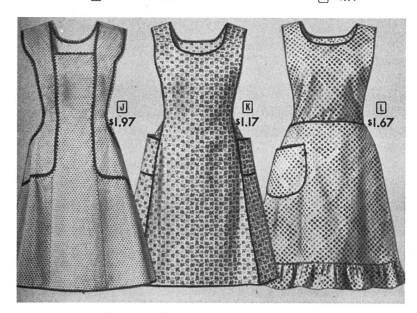

Attractive Aprons

A **Drip-dry Bib Fashion** keeps
pleats without ironing.
Printed 80-sq. percale; rick-
rack trim. Long tie-backs. Fits
up to size 20. Washable.
88 F 8538—Blue and green
88 F 8539—Yellow and orange
Shpg. wt. 7 oz....Each $1.97

B **Tiered Band Style** of washable, drip-dry 80-sq. percale combines the beauty of
pleats with the joy of knowing
you can forget about ironing.
Fits up to size 20.
88 F 8540—Red and gold paisley print. Shpg. wt. 6 oz. $1.67

C **Surplice Brunch Cobbler**..
nylon-trimmed 80-sq. per-
cale geometric print. 1 pocket.
Washable.
State bust size small (30-36);
medium (37-40); large (41-44)
in. Shipping weight 6 oz.
88 F 8536—Red on white
88 F 8537—Blue on white
Each..................$1.97

D **Pinafore Cobbler** drip-
dries. Paisley print 80-sq.
percale; solid color bib and
pocket inserts. 2-button back
closing. Washable. *State bust
size* small (30-36); medium (37-
40); large (41-44) inches.
88 F 8534—Blue and red
88 F 8535—Fuchsia and turquoise. Wt. 6 oz....Each $1.97

E **Patch Pocket Cobbler**..
washfast polished cotton.
1-button back neck closing.
Generous ties; 3 red pockets.
State bust size small (30-36); medium (37-40); large (41-44) in.
Shipping weight 6 oz.
88 F 8532—Black and white
check with red contrast.
Each...................$1.57

F **The Stole Apron!** Newest
fashion idea ties in back,
unbuttons in front so you don't
have to undo bow or mess hair
slipping it over head. Washable 80-sq. percale floral print.
Heart-shape pocket. Fits to
size 20. Shpg. wt. 4 oz.
88F8528—Red on white...$1.37
88F8529—Blue on white... 1.37

G **"Permanent K. P."** and
"Life Can Be Beautiful"
printed on pockets of candy-
striped drip-dry cotton band
styles. 1 black-and-white; 1
red-and-white. Washfast. Fit
up to size 20. Shpg. wt. 7 oz.
88 F 8533—Set of 2 for...$1.97

H **Company Mannered** band
style. Flocked floral 80-sq.
percale with white acetate-
and-nylon lace, black nylon
velvet ribbon. Washable. Fits
to size 20. Shpg. wt. 5 oz.
88 F 8530—Aqua blue...$1.97
88 F 8531—Pink........ 1.97

J **Princess cover-**
all. Full-cut 80-
sq. percale. 2 pock-
ets, long back ties.
Washfast. Shipping
weight 6 oz.
State bust size regu-
lar (32-36); large
(38-44); extra-large
(46-50) inches.
88 F 8523—Green
and white....$1.97
88 F 8524—Rose
and white....$1.97

K **Fruit-of-the-**
Loom 80-sq.
percale coverall..
trellis print on
white. 2 pockets,
back ties. Washfast.
Shpg. wt. 5 oz.
State bust size regu-
lar (30-36); large
(38-44); extra-large
(46-50) inches.
88 F 8526—Blue
88 F 8527—Red
Each........$1.17

L **Large Sizes**
will love the
colorful gaiety of
this embossed cot-
ton coverall with
ruffle trim. Long
back ties, patch
pocket. Fits bust
sizes 40 to 48
inches. Washable.
88 F 8525—Multi-
color print on
white ground.
Wt. 6 oz.....$1.67

A
$39.70
Orlon
Pile Lining
$22.70
Rayon
Pile Lining

LOVELY VERSIONS OF
the Pile Lined Coat

*.. its glamorous, wide collar
converts to a practical hood*

A **Polished Zibeline** of all wool with a white Orlon* pile lining. Sleeves are all wool interlined and lined with acetate satin. *Misses' sizes 8, 10, 12, 14, 16, 18. Please state correct size.*
T 17 F 4111—Medium blue   T 17 F 4112—Black
Shipping weight 6 lbs. 1 oz..........$4 down, Each, cash $39.70
Less expensive fabric of all wool zibeline with White Rayon Pile Lining on woven cotton back (face 50%, back 50% of total weight). Sleeves are reprocessed wool interlined and acetate taffeta lined. *State size above.* Shipping weight 5 lbs. 11 oz.
T 17 F 4123—Black...................$2.50 down; Cash $22.70

B **Corduroy.** Beige Orlon* pile lining. Sleeves are all wool interlined; rayon twill lined. *Misses' sizes 8, 10, 12, 14, 16, 18.*
T 17 F 4125—Medium beige   T 17 F 4126—Moss green (medium)
State size. Shpg. wt. 6 lbs.............$3 down; Each, cash $29.70

C **Polished Zibeline Wool Topper** lined with white rayon pile on woven cotton back (face 50%, back 50% of total wt.). About 30 in. long. Sleeves reprocessed wool interlined; acetate taffeta lined. *State Misses' size 8, 10, 12, 14, 16, 18.* Shpg. wt. 3 lbs. 11 oz.
T 17 F 4505—Black....................$2.00 down; Cash $19.70

B
$29.70

C
$19.70

* DuPont
Trade Mark
for acrylic fiber

Tie-on Scarf Hats

A The Wool Felt Cloche with blouson
crown has warm wool jersey scarf
attached . . ties front or back as you
prefer. Fits sizes 21¾ to 22½ inches.
Please state color black, light beige,
medium gray, red or navy blue.
T 78 F 8520—Shpg. wt. 12 oz. . . **$2.97**

B Wool Jersey Brim Hat combines a
favorite silhouette with protection
against cold breezes. Scarf ties front
or back. Fits 21¾ to 22½ inches.
Please state color black, medium gray,
red, gold, beige or royal blue.
T 78 F 8505—Wt. 1 lb. 2 oz. **$2.97**

C The Visor Cap . . popular, peaked
head-covering of soft wool jersey
keeps ears and neck warm despite the
winter weather. Fits all head sizes.
Please state color black, medium gray,
red, dark brown, navy blue or white.
T 78 F 8500—Shpg. wt. 9 oz. . . **$1.97**

D The Wool Jersey Scarf-Wrap has
a big shirred buttonhole to slip
the ends through. And it's self lined
for an extra little bit of warmth.
State color black, medium gray, red,
beige or white. Fits all head sizes.
T 78 F 8510—Shpg. wt. 4 oz. **$2.97**

Close-fitting Jerseys

E Winter Flower Show . . all wool
helmet completely covered over
by self-fabric blossoms centered
with decorative nailheads.
State color black, beige, gold, red
or white. Fits all head sizes.
T 78 F 8515—Shpg. wt. 3 oz. . . **$2.97**

F Deep Cloche with Tall Crown rises
to the fashion heights of the
season. All wool with grosgrain bow.
Fits size 21¾ to 22½ inches.
Please state color black, beige, medium gray, red or royal blue.
T 78 F 8535—Shpg. wt. 12 oz. **$2.47**

G Double Wool Turban . . simple yet
sophisticated headwear shirred
front and back for artful, graceful
draping. Fits all head sizes.
Please state your color choice black,
medium gray, beige, red or white.
T 78 F 8525—Shpg. wt. 3 oz. **$2.97**

H Button-on Wool Beret . . a fashion
boon for windy days because it's
held on securely under chin. Fits
head sizes 21¾ to 22½ inches.
Please state color choice black, beige,
white, red or medium gray.
T 78 F 8530—Shpg. wt. 8 oz. . . **$1.97**

Co-ordinated Sets

J Fluffy Fabric . . 38% mohair, 57% cotton, 5% nylon . . makes a match of an interesting drape-back
turban and adorable little gloves. Turban fits all head
sizes. Glove has Helanca® stretch nylon palm; fits all.
State color gold, black, lt. spice brown, royal blue.

Turban and Glove Set	*The Turban Only*
Shipping weight 5 oz.	Shipping weight 4 oz.
T 78 F 8405 . . . . **$3.97**	T 78 F 8400 . . . . **$2.47**

K Wool Jersey in Checks and Solid teams up a high-
hat turban with impish check-palmed gloves.
Fascinating fashion accent! Turban fits all head
sizes; glove fits all hand sizes. *Please state color* black
with white; red with white; or dark brown with beige.

The Turban and Glove Set	*The Turban Only*
T78F8415—Wt. 9 oz. **$3.97**	T78F8410—Wt. 8 oz. **$2.47**

HOW TO MEASURE FOR MILLINERY . . Draw
tape measure around center of forehead.
Number of inches is your correct head size

J
$3.97
Set
$2.47
Hat only

K
$3.97
Set
$2.47
Hat only

Acrilan* and wool worsteds . .

Coordinates in 70% Acrilan and 30% wool worsted . . a beautiful fabric that's washable, needs no ironing.

A *2-pc. Eton suit.* Jacket has 2 pockets. Shorts have Snugtex® elastic back waist; french fly front.
State size 1, 2, 3, 4. Shpg. wt. 1 lb. 8 oz.
29 F 9465—2 piece suit **$4.97**

B *Jumper.* Permanently-pleated skirt. Braid trim.
State size 3, 4, 5, 6, 6x.
29 F 4454—Shpg. wt. 7 oz **$3.87**

C *Blouse* in knit Acrilan. ¾-length push-up sleeves. Turtle neckline. Washable. *State* 3, 4, 5, 6, 6x. Wt. 3 oz.
29F4264—White 29F4265—Red . . Ea.**$1.67**

D *Cardigan jacket.* Braid trim. 2 pockets. Look-like-pearl buttons.
State size 3, 4, 5, 6, 6x.
29 F 4451—Shpg. wt. 7 oz **$3.87**

E *Skirt.* Permanent box pleats. Elastic back waist. Adjustable suspenders.
State size 3, 4, 5, 6, 6x.
29 F 4174—Shpg. wt. 6 oz **$2.83**

F *Tapered slacks.* Elastic back waist. 2 pockets. Button trim at bottom.
State size 3, 4, 5, 6, 6x.
29 F 4452—Shpg. wt. 6 oz **$2.83**

G *Cardigan blouse.* 100% bulky rib knit Acrilan. Long sleeves.
State size 3, 4, 5, 6, 6x. Wt. 5 oz.
29 F 4348—Red **$1.97**
*Chemstrand Reg. T.M. for acrylic fibers

Tartan Plaids

Sizes 1 to 6x

Print corduroys . .

Mix and matchers in wonderful corduroy that's washfast and easy to care for!

H *Capri pants.* Elastic back waist. 1 pocket. Slits at bottom of legs.
State size 3, 4, 5. 6 or 6x.
29 F 5938—Shpg. wt. 6 oz **$2.27**

J *Topper jacket.* Turtle neck. ¾-length raglan sleeves with button cuffs. Front belt. *State size* 3, 4, 5, 6, 6x.
29 F 5936—Shpg. wt. 6 oz **$3.57**

K *Pedal pushers.* Elastic back waist. 1 pocket. *State size* 3, 4, 5, 6, 6x.
29 F 5937—Shpg. wt. 5 oz **$1.87**

L *Blouse* in knit Acrilan. Turtle neck. ¾-length raglan sleeves. Buttons down back. *State size* 3, 4, 5, 6, 6x.
29 F 5935—White. Shpg. wt. 3 oz **$2.44**

M *Jumper.* 2 pockets. Look-like-pearl buttons. *State size* 3, 4, 5, 6, 6x.
29 F 4449—Shpg. wt. 8 oz **$2.97**

N *Blouse* in little-or-no-iron cotton. Embroidery trim on sleeves. Washable. *State size* 3, 4, 5, 6, 6x. Shpg. wt. 4 oz.
29 F 4285—White **$1.87**

P *2-piece set* for boys and girls. Knit Acrilan shirt has corduroy trim to match suspender pants. *State size* 2, 3, 4.
29 F 6789—Shpg. wt. set 12 oz **$3.87**

Really Red

A Soft-as-cashmere coat in sueded 85% wool and 15% camel's hair. Cotton velveteen collar. Rayon satin lining; reprocessed wool interlining. Dry clean.
State size 3, 4, 5, 6 or 6x.
29 F 8742—Shipping weight 2 lbs.....**$16.97**

Mother Hubbard bonnet in cotton velveteen. Softly gathered crown. Chin strap. Rayon lining. *Fits sizes 3 to 6x.*
29 F 8015—Black. Shpg. wt. 4 oz.....**$2.34**

B "Looks-like-a-jumper" dress in Wash and Wear 50% Orlon* and 50% rayon; needs little or no ironing. Cotton broadcloth collar and sleeves.
State size 3, 4, 5, 6 or 6x.
29 F 5609—Shipping weight 9 oz.....**$5.97**

C Calico print dress in little-or-no-iron cotton. White pique cuffs on ¾ length sleeves. Washable. *State size 3, 4, 5, 6 or 6x.*
29 F 5608—Shipping weight 9 oz.....**$4.97**

Leotards. Guaranteed not to run! Full-fashioned for fit. Super-soft nylon yarn. Elastic at waist. *One size fits dress sizes 3 to 6x.* Shpg. wt. 3 oz.
29F3064–Red   29 F 3065–Black..Ea. **$1.87**

Anklets. Stretch nylon. Washfast. White. Shipping weight pair 1 oz.
29 F 1954–Fits 5½–7   29 F 1955–Fits 7–8½
Pair **39c**   3 pairs for **$1.14**
*DuPont Reg. T.M. for acrylic fibers

ALL DESIGNED BY *Helen Lee*

Shine or Shower

D A washable corduroy jumper goes over the dress for a delightful combination! Moss green.
State size 3, 4, 5, 6 or 6x.
29 F 4450—Shipping wt. 9 oz.......**$3.97**

E Rain or shine coat in washable corduroy. Lined in gay calico print that matches dress (F). Matching lined bonnet. Moss green.
State size 3, 4, 5, 6 or 6x.
29 F 4694–Wt. 1 lb. 2 oz.....Coat, hat **$8.87**

Umbrella . . acetate cover. 8-rib frame, plastic handle. Shipping wt. 9 oz.
88 F 5149—Red solid
88 F 5150—Red plaid.........Each **$1.97**

F Sunny dress in little-or-no-iron cotton. Look-like pearl buttons. ¾-length sleeves. Washable.
State size 3, 4, 5, 6 or 6x.
29 F 5607—Shipping weight 8 oz.....**$4.87**

Gloves in stretch nylon, angora rabbit hair and lamb's wool. White. *One size fits 2 to 6x.*
29 F 2655—Shipping wt. pr. 1 oz.....**$1.00**

Shoes. Strap detaches underneath . . wear as strap shoe or pump. Guardtex sole.
Sizes: A (narrow) 10 to 3. Half sizes.
Sizes: C (medium) 8½ to 3. Half sizes.
State size, width. Shpg. wt. 1 lb. 6 oz.
15 F 1186A—Black nylon velvet...Pair **$4.77**
15 F 1184A—Red leather (C width only)
15 F 1183A—Black patent......Pair **$4.77**

KERRY-TEEN

E
$4.77
Orlon*-Wool

J
$4.84
Jacket
Was $5.40

F
$3.97
Rayon-Wool

K
$1.47
Shirt

←G
$2.97
Corduroy

L
$2.77
Pullover

H $3.64 Corduroy
Was $3.94

M $2.26 Pullover

N
$11.90

P
$6.60

A Slacks $2.94
B Shirt $1.97

C Slacks $4.60
D Car Coat $9.90

Ivy League Coordinates

Here's the famous styling teens love so well, in meant-for-each-other cottons. *Sizes 10, 12, 14, 16. Please state size.*

A **Slacks** of corded cotton have hip flaps, side pocket and zipper, tapered legs. Belt not included. Washable; max. fabric shrinkage 1%.
77 F 8143–Lt. blue.   77 F 8142–Black
77 F 8141–Beige.. Wt. 11 oz. Ea. $2.94

B **Roll-up Sleeve Shirt** in a glowing plaid. Washable, Sanforized . . fabric won't shrink over 1%.
77 F 7729–Red. Shpg. wt. 4 oz..$1.97
77 F 7730–Blue. Shpg. wt. 4 oz.. 1.97

Checkered Partners

Subtle-toned hound's-tooth check in corduroy and contrasting solid poplin form a smart sportswear ensemble. *Sizes 10, 12, 14, 16. Please state size.*

C **Princess-waist Slacks.** Tunnel belt loops, self belt. Side pocket. Washable corduroy. Shpg. wt. 11 oz.
77 F 8105—Red and gray...... $4.60

D **Car Coat** of Impregnole-finished cotton poplin. Checked corduroy trim, hood lining. Rayon lining, quilted to 100% reprocessed wool interlining. Dry clean. Wt. 1 lb. 14 oz.
77 F 8106—Beige..............$9.90

Separates

that stress the slim line for a young miss

N $2.97

L $9.94 2-pc. Suit

K $6.97 3-pc. Set

M $5.97

J $7.94

P $4.54 Skirt

R $2.74 Blouse

H $4.97 Reversible

H

T $8.90 2-pc. Set

S $8.90 2-pc. Set

Ballet Slipper Charm Bracelet . . points to her heart. *State* gold or silver color. Wt. 2 oz.
4 F 3830E—7¼-inch.
Bracelet......$1.00
10% Fed. Tax incl.

PCBKMN 2 SEARS

the Boy-coat

100% Imported Menswear Camel's Hair

Our exclusive Mary Lewis classic . . impeccably styled with fine hand-stitched detail, soft rounded lapels, traditional back belt, fly-buttoned back vent. Handsome stay-back bone buttons; inside button closings to assure perfect drape. Lined in Milium insulated acetate satin. Shpg. wt. 4 lbs. 7 oz.
Fits Juniors and Misses . . State size
7–8, 9–10, 11–12, 13–14, 15–16, 17–18.
T 17 F 2375—Camel tan
T 17 F 2376—Navy blue
$5 down . . . . .Each, cash **$49.00**

75% Wool, 25% Camel's Hair . .
Milium insulated acetate satin lined.
Fits Juniors and Misses . . State size
7–8, 9–10, 11–12, 13–14, 15–16, 17–18.
Shipping weight 5 pounds 1 ounce.
T 17 F 2378—Camel tan
T 17 F 2379—Navy blue
$3 down . . . . .Each, cash **$29.00**

Orlon* Pile Zip-out Liner . . 75% wool, 25% camel's hair. Lined with acetate satin.
Fits Juniors and Misses . . State size
7–8, 9–10, 11–12, 13–14, 15–16, 17–18. Shipping weight 6 pounds.
T 17 F 4238–Camel tan; tan pile
T 17 F 4239–Navy blue; white pile
$3.50 down . . . . .Each, cash **$34.70**

6-Footer Scarf . . a vivid stroke of virgin wool tubular knit. About 9x72 in. including fringe. Hand wash separately. From Japan. Shpg. wt. 7 oz.
88 F 8977–Red and white stripe **$2.97**
88 F 8978–Royal blue and white **2.97**

* DuPont trademark
for acrylic fiber

her *Blazer*

Pure Wool of a very fine quality, impeccably tailored with hand picked stitching around the lapels and pockets. An unusual imported Indian emblem and brass coin buttons add a distinctive touch. Fully rayon lined. About 26 inches long. Dry clean. *State size.*
Misses' sizes 8, 10, 12, 14, 16, 18. Shpg. wt. 1 lb. 4 oz.
T7 F 1310—White. . **$17.90**

Pleated Skirt . . perfect companion for the blazer! The fabric is a soft, lovely flannel of imported English lamb's wool. Stitched from waist to hipline, graceful, crisp pleats fall in flattering precision. Side zipper. Dry clean. For knee socks, see page 7.
Misses' sizes 8, 10, 12, 14, 16, 18. *Please state size.*
T7 F 4577—Medium gray
Shpg. wt. 1 lb. 8 oz.. **$12.94**

his *Sport Coat*

Styled for leisure in a handsome self-textured fabric loomed of 95% virgin wool, 5% nylon. 3-button rayon-lined model with welt seams, flap pockets, side vents. *State chest size, height and weight.*
Shorts 36 to 42 in. *Regulars* 35 to 46 in. *Longs* 37 to 46 in.
T 45 F 1740—Dark blue
T 45 F 1760—Natural (tan)
T 45 F 1790—Dark brown
Shpg. wt. 3 lbs. 2 oz. **$24.50**

Slacks. Premium quality 100% virgin wool flannel. Double pleats, continuous waistband; zipper fly. Waist sizes 28 to 42 inches. Inseam sizes 28 to 35 inches. *State height, waist and inseam; indicate waist.* Shipping weight 1 lb. 12 oz.
T 45 F 8231—Medium gray
T 45 F 8238—Brown. **$14.50**
Save $1.50 on 2-piece Outfit.
Shpg. wt. 4 lbs. 8 oz.
T 45 F 4026 . . . . **$37.50**

PCBKMN
AMDSLG 2 **SEARS**

Dirty Bucks with Shu-Lok® Fastener

G · White or dirty buck

H · Black or dirty buck

F

BUCKS

$8⁹⁷ CHOICE OF 3 STYLES

F **London Gray,** the new fashionable color for popular Bucks. Black rubber sole, heel. Pacifate twill vamp lining. Flexible Goodyear welt.
Sizes: D (medium) width in 6½, 7, 7½, 8, 8½, 9, 9½, 10, 10½, 11 and 12.
Sizes: EE (wide) width in 7½, 8, 8½, 9, 9½, 10, 10½. *State size and width.*
Shipping weight 2 lbs. 14 oz.
67 F 4174—Dark gray.........Pair **$8.97**

G **Snowy White or Dirty Buck** brushed (suede) leather. Red rubber sole, heel. Pacifate vamp lining.
Sizes: B (narrow) width in 8½, 9, 9½, 10, 10½, 11. *State size, width.*
Sizes: D (medium) width 6½, 7, 7½, 8, 8½, 9, 9½, 10, 10½, 11 and 12.
Sizes: EE (wide) width in 7½, 8, 8½, 9, 9½, 10, 10½. *State size and width.*
Shipping weight 2 lbs. 14 oz.
67 F 4149—White............Pair **$8.97**
67 F 4144—Dirty buck (light tan)..Pair **8.97**

H **Convenient Shu-Lok® Fastener** shoes. No wonder they're so popular . . flip, they open; snap, they close. Dirty Buck (lt. tan) brushed (suede) leather, or smooth black leather. Dirty Bucks have black SEAROFOAM sole, heel. Smooth leather have rubber sole, heel; leather storm welt. Pacifate vamp linings, Goodyear welts.
Sizes: B (narrow) width 8, 8½, 9, 9½, 10, 10½, 11. *State size and width.*
Sizes: D (medium) 7, 7½, 8, 8½, 9, 9½, 10, 10½, 11, 12. *State size, width.*
67 F 4280—Black. Wt. 3 lbs. 4 oz.
67 F 4266—Dirty buck. Wt. 2 lbs. 14 oz.
Pair...................................**$8.97**

CHUKKA BOOTS

$10⁷⁶ $8⁷⁰

J **Keep your feet warm** and protected this winter. This smart new nylon-fleece lined boot caresses feet in deep, cozy comfort. Ankle-high brushed (suede) leather uppers in the new London gray color . . they're easy-bending, scuff resistant. Cushiony, long-wearing SEAROFOAM sole, heel. Goodyear welt construction.
Sizes: D (medium) in 7½, 8, 8½, 9, 9½, 10, 10½, 11, 12. *Please state size wanted.* Shipping weight 2 lbs. 12 oz.
67 F 4077—Dk. gray. Pair **$10.76**

K **Year after year** this desert-inspired styling stays popular. It's good-looking, practical, but that's not the whole story. The soft, brushed leather molds gently to your feet. The genuine plantation crepe sole is lightweight, springy. In new London gray or sand.
Sizes: D (medium) width in 7, 7½, 8, 8½, 9, 9½, 10, 10½, 11 and 12. *Please state size.* Shpg. wt. 2 lbs. 12 oz.
67 F 4075—Sand color
67 F 4076—London (dark) gray
Pair..................**$8.70**

J

K · Sand or London gray

Continental is the word for these easy-wearing outfits

A **Jacquard Pattern Sweater** . . intricate Scandinavian-influenced design. 75% lamb's wool, 25% Orlon* . . . soft, lightweight, yet warm. Highly popular shawl collar . . . double-thick and bulky knit. Hand wash separately. *State* small (34–36-in. chest), med. (38–40), large (42–44). Wt. 1 lb. 12 oz.

33 F1963—Green   33 F1965—Lt. gray
33 F1964—Charcoal gray. Each **$8.97**

B **Slacks.** Latest sport model with new slanted "continental" side pockets. Wash and Wear 70% Acrilan†, 30% rayon flannel. Plain front, beltless extension waistband; adjustable side tabs. Back flap pockets; zipper. *State height, waist, inseam. Sizes on chart "C," page 652.* Wt. 1 lb. 12 oz.

45 F 6961—Medium gray
45 F 6962—Charcoal gray. Each **$7.90**

C **Matching Jacquard Pattern Socks.** 100% hi-bulk Orlon. Slack length; elastic top. Nylon-reinforced heel, toe. *State* green, charcoal gray. *State size* 10½, 11, 11½, 12, 13.

83 F 1918—Shpg. wt. pr. 2 oz. Pair **97c**
* DuPont Reg. T.M. for acrylic fiber
† Chemstrand Reg. T.M. for acrylic fiber

D **Boat-neck "Shaggy" Sweater.** 75% lamb's wool, 25% Orlon . . . light, warm. Brushed to give soft coloring and "hairy" texture. Generous full sleeves. Hand wash separately. *State size from (A) at left.* Shipping weight 1 pound 6 ounces.

33 F 1960—Charcoal brown heather
33 F 1961—Charcoal red heather
33 F 1959—Gray heather. Each **$6.90**

E **Slacks.** Top-fashion "hopsack" in a Wash and Wear blend of 70% Acrilan, 30% rayon. Trim "campus" model with plain front, square-flap back pockets; zipper. Nylon trim. *State height, waist, inseam. See chart "C," page 652 for sizes.* Wt. 1 lb. 12 oz.

45 F 5939—Olive
45 F 5938—Brown
45 F 5932—Charcoal gray. Each **$5.74**

F **Soft Matching "Shaggy" Socks.** Rib knit solid colors of 100% Orlon. Slack length; elastic top. Nylon-reinforced heel, toe. *State color* gray heather, brown heather. *State size* 10½, 11, 11½, 12, 13.

83 F 1920—Shpg. wt. pr. 2 oz. Pair **97c**

G **Continental-style Boat-neck Sweater.** Knit of fine 100% virgin wool worsted. Robust heavyweight big-stitch knit gives expensive hand-knit look. Fine stitch at sides and side vents adds an extra stylish touch. Hand wash separately. *State size from (A) at far left.* Shpg. wt. 2 lbs.

33 F 1966—Blue   33 F 1967—White
33 F 1968—Black . . . . . . Each **$12.97**

H **Slacks.** Our best wool worsted flannels—imported from Japan! Precision-cut, hand tailored, hand finished. New model with latest inverted pleat styling, beltless extension waistband; adjustable side tabs. Zipper. *State height, waist and inseam. See chart "A", page 652 for sizes.* Wt. 1 lb. 14 oz.

T45 F 9221—Medium gray
T45 F 9222—Charcoal gray. Ea. **$17.50**

J **Matching Virgin Wool Socks.** Solid colors in warm, resilient rib knit . . . treated to retard shrinkage. Slack length; elastic top. Nylon-reinforced heel, toe. *State color* light blue, black. *State size* 10½, 11, 11½, 12, 13.

83 F 1919—Shpg. wt. pr. 2 oz. Pair **97c**

Set-ups...

Imported Shell Cordovans

New from England . . finest cordovan leather. Fully leather lined. Double leather sole, leather heel with metal V-plate.

Sizes: B (narrow) 9 to 11, 12, 13.
Sizes: C (med. narrow) 8 to 11, 12.
Sizes: D (medium) 7 to 11, 12, 13.

Half sizes too (no 11½, 12½). *State size, width.* Wt. 2 lbs. 8 oz.

T 67 F 4447A—Cordovan.Pr .**$14.90**
T 67 F 4448A—Black. . Pair **14.90**

Set-up for style and warmth

100% Lamb's Wool Coat-Sweater. Button-front. Shawl collar. Hand washable. *State size* small (36–38-in. chest), medium (40–42), large (44–46). See measuring instructions on page 699. Shipping weight 1 pound 8 ounces.
33 F 2200—Black   33 F 2201—Light Oxford gray
33 F 2202—Dark Brown . . . . .Each **$8.90**

Bulky-knit Combed Cotton Crew Socks. Striped Morpul® elastic top. Washfast. *State color* black or brown. *State size* 10, 10½, 11, 11½, 12, 13.
83 F 1917—Shipping weight pair 3 ounces . . . . . .Pair **87c**

Campus Styled Corduroy Suit

A unique coat. slack and vest combination in vertical-wale corduroy. 3-button single-breasted coat has patch pockets with flaps; fancy rayon lining; brass color buttons. Corduroy vest reverses to fancy patterned rayon which matches coat lining. Vest has 6-button front, brass color buttons; 2 pockets (on each side) with imitation flaps. Unpleated trousers have square-flap back pockets; zipper fly. *State chest, waist, inseam; height and weight.* **Regulars** 35 to 42 in. **Longs** 37 to 42 in. Shpg. wt. 6 lbs.
T 45 F 4099—Tan   T 45 F 4059—Olive **$24.50**

in any league

Check Shirt and Belt

Shirt. Short point regular spread collar . . permanent stays. 1-button flap pocket. Box pleat front. Minimum care combed cotton. Washable. *State* small (14–14½-in. neck), medium (15–15½), large (16–16½), extra large (17–17½).
33 F 562—Wt. 1 lb. . .Each **$2.90**

Matching Fabric Belt . . 1 in. wide. Adjustable . . fits sizes 28 to 40.
33 F 4222—Wt. 4 oz.. Each **$1.40**

Lustrous Bedford Cords

Smartly styled 8-ounce all-season weight combed cotton in a handsome ribbed weave. Slim, trim model features small side-straps below waist plus flaps on hip pockets. All combed yarns for lasting luster, long wear. Wash and Wear, needs little or no ironing. Maximum fabric shrinkage 1%. Smart plain front. No belt. Order belt shown above. *Please state waist and inseam; see chart below. Tell which is waist.* Shipping weight 1 pound.

41 F 7785—Natural tan
41 F 7786—Charcoal (dark) gray
41 F 7787—Ice (light) blue
41 F 7788—Olive gray **$4.70**

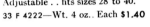

Size Chart for Bedford Cords	
Waist, inches	Inseam, inches
29, 30, 31; 33; 38	. . . . .29 to 32
32, 34, 36	. . . . .29 to 34
40.	. . . . .29, 30, 32

Smart Sport Combination

Sport Coat. An attractive miniature print pattern in popular vertical-wale corduroy. Vinyl trimmed pockets. Rayon-lined, 3-button, flap-pocket model.
State chest size. **Regulars** 36, 37, 38, 39, 40; 42, 44, 46 in. **Longs** 37, 38, 39, 40; 42, 44, 46 in. Shpg. wt. 2 lbs. 15 oz.

T45F1210—Gray **T45F1270**—Brown.**$15.60**

Slacks. Wash and Wear flannel of 70% Acrilan*, 30% rayon. Continuous waistband, pleats, zipper. *State height, waist, inseam.* Waist 28 to 42 in. Inseam 28 to 35 in. Shpg. wt. 1 lb. 12 oz.

45F5232—Dk. gray **45F5238**—Brown .**$5.90**

Save $1.00 on 2-pc. Outfit. *State sizes and colors.* Shpg. wt. 4 lbs. 5 oz.

T 45 F 4025—Coat and Slacks . . . **$20.50**

* Chemstrand Reg. T.M. for acrylic fiber

Belles and Beaus go Formal

Pleated white Formal Shirt. 2x2 imported cotton broadcloth front, combed batiste body. Soft collar. French cuffs. *State neck, sleeve size.*
33 F 190—Shpg. wt. 1 lb. $4.94

Neck size	Sleeve size	Neck size	Sleeve size
14½	32–33	16	32–33–34–35
15	32–33–34	16½	32–33–34–35
15½	32–33–34–35		

Man's Dress Jewelry. Genuine smoke colored Mother of Pearl links, studs set into yellow gold plate. Fashion correct for your tuxedo. Gift boxed.
4F1599E—Cuff links and 3 studs. Wt. 4 oz. Set $5.50

Clip-on Bow Tie and Cummerbund. Rayon Barathea. *State color* black, maroon, midnight blue. *State size* extra small (25½–29½-in. waist), small (29½–33½), medium (33½–37½).
33 F 4000—Shpg. wt. 10 oz. ....Set $3.94

Her Shoes, of dyeable white rayon satin. Guardtex sole, and little 2-inch heel. *State size, width.*
Sizes: AA (narrow) width in 7, 7½, 8, 8½ and 9.
Sizes: B (medium) 5,5½,6, 6½,7,7½,8,8½,9,9½,10.
T 54 F 8449A—Shpg. wt. 1 lb. 9 oz. .....Pair $5.74

Her Capeskin Shortie Glove. Half pique seams, button closing inside wrist. About 8-in. long. Hand wash alone. *State size* 6, 6½, 7, 7½, 8. Shpg. wt. 3 oz.
88 F 5746—White $3.97   88 F 5745—Black $3.97

Glamorous Acetate Satin Bolero. Covered buttons, ¾ set-in sleeves; acetate taffeta lining. Dry clean. *State size* small (fits 7-9); medium (fits 11-13); large (fits 15-17). Shpg. wt. 1 lb. 1 oz.
88 F 8989—Cranberry red.................$5.97
88 F 8990—Teal blue.................... 5.97

Acetate Satin Head-bows are attached to self-covered clips that fit everyone. You get 1 cranberry red, 1 teal blue (colors to match bolero).
88 F 8804—Shipping weight 4 oz. .Set of **2** for $1.97

Long-stemmed Roses on a floating cloud . . a dress of pure enchantment. Filmy nylon, crisp and smooth as organdy, bordered with flocked roses. Lightly boned bodice with cuff and bow in front. Harem skirt over nylon net . . full lining of acetate taffeta. Long back zipper. Dry clean. *Order correct size.*
Juniors' sizes 5, 7, 9, 11, 13, 15.

T 31 F 08005—Pink trim on pink
T 31 F 08006—Pink trim on white
T 31 F 08007—Yellow trim on yellow
Shipping weight 2 lbs. .....Each $16.50

Tuxedo. (Coat and trousers). Woven of tropical rayon and Dacron. Flap-pockets, rayon-satin shawl collar. Center vent. Full rayon lining. Pleated trousers have rayon-satin braid trim, suspender buttons; zipper fly.
State chest, waist, inseam; height, weight.
Shorts 36 to 42 in. **Reg.** 35 to 46 in. **Longs** 36 to 46 in. *Waist sizes* 27 to 43 in. *Inseam sizes* 28 to 35 in. Shpg. wt. 5 lbs.
T 45 F 53962—Blue-black........$39.50

Our Best Tuxedo of tropical weight wool worsted. Same sizes and style as above.

Dancing Ensemble in a finely ribbed white faille (rayon and cotton). Princess dress has a lined bodice of pale blue or pale pink acetate satin . . back zipper. Lace flowers and glitter glamorize the lined jacket. Dry clean. *State size.*
Juniors' sizes 7, 9, 11, 13, 15.
⊤ 31 F 8023—White with blue
⊤ 31 F 8024—White with pink
Shpg. wt. 2 lbs. . 2-pc. **$15.00**

Bouffant Dress, charmingly bow-accented . . in vibrantly-hued sheer silk organza over acetate taffeta. Skirt has wide band around back, 5-inch hem. Long back zipper. Dry clean. *State size.*
Juniors' sizes 5, 7, 9, 11, 13, 15.
⊤ 31 F 8082—Flamingo pink
⊤ 31 F 8083—Peacock blue
⊤ 31 F 8084—Royal blue
Wt. 1 lb. 6 oz. . . . .Each **$16.50**

Glamorous Evening Coat of acetate satin. Pretty collar perks high . . irrepressible flare assured by interfacing of Inter-lon (cotton, rayon and acetate bonded together). Self-fabric buttons and bow. Lined in white acetate satin.
State Juniors' size 5, 7, 9, 11, 13, 15. Shpg. wt. 3 lbs. 12 oz.
⊤ 17 F 6584—Black
$2.50 down . . . . .Cash **$24.70**

''Ball of Fire'' aurora jewelry. *State* gold color with ruby aurora; rhodium with sapphire aurora or crystal aurora.
4 F 3860E—15 in. Necklace, earring. Wt. 2 oz. **$1.98**
4 F 3861E—Wt. 2 oz. Bracelet 7¼ in. **1.00**
10% Fed. Tax incl.

it's real
RACCOON

[A] **The Newest-looking Topper** has a marvelous raccoon collar and a lining of warm Orlon* pile. The fabric . . a fine blend of 75% wool, 25% camel's hair. About 32 inches long. Sleeves lined in reprocessed wool quilted to acetate taffeta. See glove section for gloves. Boots sold on page 11. Wt. 3 lbs. 7 oz. *Fits Juniors and Misses 5–6, 7–8, 9–10, 11–12, 13–14, 15–16. State size.*
T 17 F 06403—Camel tan; beige pile
T 17 F 06404—Red; beige pile
$3 down . . . . Each, cash **$29.90**

[B] **Poplin Coat** wins new popularity with its big raccoon collar, wonderful Orlon* pile lining. In fine, water-repellent cotton. Sleeves lined with reprocessed wool quilted to acetate taffeta. *Fits Juniors' and Misses'. State size 5–6, 7–8, 9–10, 11–12, 13–14, 15–16, 17–18.* Shipping wt. 4 lbs.
T 17 F 06310—Loden green; black pile
T 17 F 06311—Beige; beige pile
T 17 F 06312—Black; black pile
$2.50 down . . . . Each, cash **$24.90**

Fashion Boot of water-repellent cotton corduroy is lined with rayon fleece pile. Wear over stocking foot. Vulcanized ribbed rubber sole. Shpg. wt. 1 lb. 10 oz.
Sizes: C medium wide) 5, 6, 7, 8, 9. *For half sizes, order half size larger. State size.*
76 F 9544A—Red . . . . Pair $5.74
76 F 9545A—Black . . . . Pair 5.74

Huge Tote Bag of leather-like plastic stashes books, gloves, kerchiefs. Gold-color disc turn-lock. Rear wall and inner zip pockets; plastic lining. About 12½x12 inches. Includes 10% Fed. Excise Tax.
88 F 876E—Med. tan. Wt. 2 lbs. 8 oz.$5.57
88 F 875E—Red. Shpg. wt. 2 lbs. 8 oz. 5.57

* DuPont trademark for acrylic fiber

V-Neck Pullover, indispensable to a good casual wardrobe. 88% Australian wool, 10% kid mohair, 2% Shetland wool. Hand washable. For shirt-dickey see index; for pin, page 25B. *State size 34, 36, 38, 40. Shpg. wt. 12 oz.*
T7 F 9851—Charcoal gray heather...... $5.94
T7 F 9852—Black.......................... 5.94

"Ancient Tartan" Plaid, a fashion fabric of 100% imported wool, a must in your new Fall skirt plan. Slim and smooth . . partly lined. Self belt; back zip. Dry clean. Shpg. wt. 1 lb. 4 oz.
State Misses' size 8, 10, 12, 14, 16, 18.
T7 F 4636—Wine, gold and green plaid... $9.90

Bulky Turtleneck Pullover, a dashing casual with sporty ways, great fashion impact. A fine attention-getter in a bold all-over cable-stitch pattern. 100% virgin wool. Hand washable. *State size 34, 36, 38, 40. Shpg. wt. 1 lb. 4 oz.*
T7 F 9883—Gold   T7 F 9882—White
T7 F 9884—Black   Each......... $9.97

Walking Shorts of fine imported 100% wool flannel. Sleekly styled with a zippered fly front, a neat self fabric belt. Convenient pair of side seam pockets. Dry clean. Shpg. wt. 9 oz.
Junior sizes 7, 9, 11, 13, 15. State size.
T7 F 6467—Oxford medium gray...... $7.74

Initial Pendant. Personalized with your own initial or can be used for school letter. Large 2-in. satin finish block initial on 20-in. link chain. *State initial;* all letters exc. Q,U,X,Y,Z. In burnished gold color. 10% Tax incl.
4 F 3853E—Wt. 3 oz...... $1.00

Suede Handbag folds over or is a tote. Top-grain lambskin, rayon-lined. Gold-color finger grip. About 9¼x5 inches. Shipping weight 13 ounces.
88 F 742E—Green........ $3.97
88 F 740E—Fawn (tan).... 3.97
88 F 741E—Red.......... 3.97

Suede Flattie has bright brass trim! Guardtex sole, ½-inch heel. *Sizes:* AA(narrow) 7,7½,8,8½,9. *Sizes:* B (medium) width 5, 5½, 6, 6½, 7, 7½, 8, 8½, 9. *State size,* width. Shpg. wt. 1 lb. 8 oz.
54 F 8061–Red 54 F 8063–Green
54 F 8062–Fawn (tan) Pair $4.77

Coat alone $16.67 Coat and slacks $18.67 Coat alone $13.67 Coat and slacks $19.67 Coat, cap, slacks $18.67 Coat and cap $13.67

CLASSICS .. coats with a tailored look

A large fluffy shawl collar that looks just like raccoon (made of dyed imported lamb) highlights this luxurious classic coat styled to delight any little lady. Soft, sueded 85% wool and 15% camel hair is exquisitely tailored into a boxy double-breasted style. Fashionwise belted back and two stitched flap pockets. Fully lined in rayon; interlined with warm reprocessed wool. Dry clean only.
Please state size 4, 5, 6, 6x.
29 F 8738—Camel
29 F 8739—Red
Shipping weight 2 lbs............$16.67

The ever-popular "Boy Coat" in a luxurious blend of 85% wool and 15% camel hair . . . a fashionable flatterer for every little girl. Convertible collar buttons under chin for added cold weather protection. Belted back with inverted pleat. Iridescent rayon taffeta lining; warm reprocessed wool interlining. Lined slacks. Dry clean.
State size 4, 5, 6, 6x.
29 F 8629—Navy **29 F 8628**—Camel
Shpg. wt. set 3 lbs. 8 oz......set $18.67
Coat alone. Shpg. wt. 1 lb. 13 oz.
29 F 8705—Navy **29 F 8704**—Camel
Coat alone...................$13.67

A stunning style
Deftly tailored in a luxurious basket weave of 100% wool. Highly styled with large cotton velveteen framed collar fashioned to flatter any little girl. Inverted side pleats with bow ties. Inverted back pleat with flange across back waist. Large novelty buttons provide smart accent. Fully rayon lined; warm reprocessed wool interlining. Dry clean only.
State size 4, 5, 6, 6x. Shipping weight set 2 pounds.
29 F 8651—Neon (medium) blue
29 F 8650—Red...Coat and slacks $19.67

Boys' regulation coat set superbly tailored in all wool melton. Gleaming brass-colored buttons. Deftly styled with notched lapels and a belted back. Plaid Chromspun acetate lining; warm reprocessed wool interlining. Fully rayon lined Eton cap with inband and chin strap completes this smart set. Slacks have adjustable suspenders, cotton kasha lining. Dry clean only. Shipping weight set 3 lbs.
State size 3, 4, 5, 6, 6x.
29 F 8945—Coat, slacks, cap.....$18.67
Coat and cap only. Shpg. wt. 2 lbs.
29 F 8872....................$13.67

Fall's smartest millinery styled in soft cotton velveteen. Chic roller hat features a beautifully finished stitched brim and pert rayon grosgrain ribbon streamer and chin strap. Double thick cotton velveteen ear flaps provide cozy warmth for chilly winter days. *State color* brown, navy or red. *State size* small (fits 19 inches), medium (20 inches), large (21 inches). To measure, draw tape around head above ears. Number of inches is correct size.
29 F 8019—Shipping weight 4 ounces...$2.34

	Measuring Chart for Coats, Sizes 3 to 6x				
	Size is......	...3....	...4....	...5....	...6....	...6x.....
Order only sizes listed with each catalog number.	If height is...	34½–37	37½–40	40½–43	43½–46	46½–48 inches
	If chest is.....	..22...	..23...	..24...	..25...	..25½ inches..
	If weight is..	29½–34	34½–38	38½–44	44½–49	49½–54 pounds
	Coat length..	..20...	..21½..	..22½..	..24½..	..26 inches...